THE DOCTOR WITHIN: HOW THE MIND SHAPES CHRONIC ILLNESS

RAKESH THESIA

Dedication

To Dr. Vrajlal Mehta,
my esteemed teacher and mentor.
Your depth of knowledge, integrity, and tireless
commitment to the art of healing have profoundly
influenced my professional and personal path. It is with
great respect and heartfelt appreciation that I dedicate
this work to you.

Contents

Contents

Preface

Although I was formally trained and qualified as a homoeopathic physician, my early years of medical practice began in a rather conventional manner, as a General Practitioner primarily managing acute and seasonal illnesses. In those initial stages, my clinical approach largely mirrored that of other physicians: taking detailed notes on physical symptoms, recommending standard diagnostic tests, and prescribing medicines accordingly. Some patients recovered quickly, while others showed little to no improvement, and I often found myself questioning the limitations of this surface-level approach.

However, over time, my practice began to evolve. A growing number of patients suffering from chronic conditions started seeking my help. Patients are burdened not just by persistent symptoms but by an inner hope for something deeper, something beyond conventional treatment. Despite my best efforts, I realized that I was offering little more than temporary relief, not true healing. I was treating bodies, but not the whole person.

Then came the transformative year of 2021 and the global COVID-19 pandemic. That period of crisis became an unexpected turning point in both my professional journey and personal understanding of health. Through direct encounters with patients, as well as my own experience with the virus, I began to observe startling patterns. Some individuals, despite severe lung involvement, recovered smoothly, while others with seemingly mild symptoms deteriorated rapidly. These inconsistencies couldn't be explained by physical pathology alone.

During the isolation period, I immersed myself in deep study and reflection. Drawing from my roots in homoeopathy, I began exploring the often-overlooked psychological and emotional dimensions of disease. I integrated mind-based therapeutic approaches along with homoeopathic principles and started applying them with sincerity and attention. The results were astonishing. Patients with chronic, stubborn conditions began to show remarkable improvement, both physically and emotionally.

This book is a reflection of that journey. It offers a focused exploration into the psychological factors that significantly influence chronic illness, these factors often underestimated or neglected in mainstream medicine. While the scope of mind-body medicine is vast, this work attempts to shine a light on some of the most impactful emotional patterns I have encountered in my clinical practice. It is not meant as a comprehensive manual, but rather as an invitation to look deeper, to understand the human being behind the disease, and to consider a more integrated approach to healing.

Acknowledgements

With deep gratitude and humility, I extend my heartfelt thanks to all those who have shaped the journey that led to the creation of this book.

With profound humility and gratitude, I begin by offering my deepest thanks to the Almighty, whose grace, guidance, and presence have illuminated my path at every stage of life. It is through divine will and strength that this book has come into existence, and I remain ever grateful for the inner peace, clarity, and purpose bestowed upon me.

I am eternally indebted to my parents, whose unwavering love, values, and sacrifices laid the foundation for everything I have achieved. Their guidance and encouragement have been the silent force behind every step I have taken, and their belief in me has been a constant source of strength.

To my beloved wife, thank you for your patience, support, and understanding throughout this journey. Your companionship and quiet resilience have been my anchor during the most challenging moments. Without your presence and encouragement, this endeavor would not have been possible.

I also wish to express sincere appreciation to all my teachers and mentors, whose wisdom, discipline, and inspiration have profoundly shaped my professional and personal growth. Their teachings have not only informed my knowledge but also instilled in me a deep sense of purpose and responsibility as a healer and writer.

Most importantly, I dedicate my gratitude to my patients, who have been my greatest teachers. Through their stories, struggles, and healing journeys, I have learned more about the complexities of life, health, and the human spirit than any textbook could ever convey. Their trust and openness have enriched my understanding and inspired the insights shared in this book.

To all of you, thank you for being an integral part of this journey.

Introduction

The Illness Beneath the Surface

I still remember the day that changed everything.

It was a hot, ordinary afternoon in my clinic in Gujarat. The waiting room was full, and the routine cases kept coming, like diabetes, high blood pressure, arthritis, asthma, URTI, gastroenteritis etc....I was doing general practice using allopathic medicine in spite of studying in homoeopathy. Seeing 10 to 15 patients in an hour, my clinic work was just concentrated on signs and symptoms with lab reports. But that day, one patient stopped me in my tracks. A woman in her late forties came in with persistent back pain, fatigue, and a dull sadness in her eyes. I had seen her before, given the necessary medicine, advised tests, and yet nothing had improved. Her reports were largely normal, her spine showed no damage, and yet her suffering was real.

Something told me to pause that day. To not just ask, "Where does it hurt?" but instead, "What's hurting you in life?"

She looked at me, stunned at first. Then her eyes welled up. Slowly, words tumbled out: about her loneliness, a cold marriage, an unfulfilled life. That consultation didn't end with a prescription. It ended with something more powerful, listening.

I have learned about psychosomatic causes of illness in medical school but that was the moment I truly understood: **not all illnesses are physical**. Some are buried in the mind, stored in memories, unspoken emotions, and silent trauma.

As a doctor trained in both modern and homoeopathic medicine, I was taught to examine symptoms, run tests, prescribe drugs, and follow protocols. But as a homoeopath I was also taught how **the human mind—its beliefs, thoughts, and suppressed emotions—could shape health more profoundly than any physical cause**.

Since my college days, I have had more interests in the role of psychology in different human endeavors. Healing is one of them.I have read numerous books on mind, attended various seminars on power of subconscious mind and attended multiple sessions of different meditation techniques, healing techniques, NLP etc. But among them Vipassana meditation inspires me to dig deeper in the subject. I started gathering all knowledge acquired upon the subject of mind power and practical experiences of my clinical practice give me insight to write this book.

Over the years, I began noticing patterns. Patients with persistent diseases often carried emotional burdens: grief that never healed, guilt that lingered for years, relationships that drained them, or childhood wounds they never spoke about. These were not just side stories, they were the roots of disease.

Science is catching up too. Fields like psychoneuroimmunology and epigenetics now show how the mind and emotions directly affect our immunity, hormones, and even gene expression. What ancient wisdom and healing traditions have long known, modern research is now proving.

This book is my journey, both as a doctor and a fellow human being into understanding how **the mind can both create and heal chronic illness**. It's filled with real stories from my practice, personal reflections, and practical tools that I've seen help people reclaim their health, not just by treating the body, but by healing the mind.

If you or someone you love has been struggling with a chronic illness, this book is my heartfelt offering. It's not just about medicine. It's about meaning. About reconnecting with the parts of ourselves we've ignored, repressed, or forgotten and realizing that perhaps the most powerful healer we've been looking for is the one within.

Welcome to The Doctor Within.

Let's begin.

CHAPTER I

My Wake-Up Call

A Case That Haunts Me Still

Her name was Rita (name changed, all names are changed in this book), a 42-year-old schoolteacher with a soft-spoken manner and eyes that carried more fatigue than her words ever could. When she first came into my clinic, she complained of body-wide pain, unrelenting tiredness, and erratic menstrual cycles. Her history was long, peppered with visits to general physicians, orthopedists, gynecologists, and alternative healers. The diagnosis, after much trial and error, was fibromyalgia. But a diagnosis is only a label, it doesn't explain why. That was the question haunting both her and me.

"Nothing works," she said, her voice barely audible, staring at her lap. "I feel like I'm going crazy."

All her reports were deceptively normal. Hemoglobin, thyroid panel, vitamin D, autoimmune markers, all within accepted medical parameters. To a casual observer, she was a perfectly healthy woman. But I saw something else, an invisible burden clinging to her like a second skin. Her posture was rigid. Her fingers clutched her handbag as if it were the last thread holding her together.

I paused. For once, I didn't reach for the prescription pad. Instead, I asked a question as I learned in homoeopathic medical school:

"Rita, when did all of this begin? What was happening in your life at the time?"

She blinked, startled. No one had asked her that before. After a long silence, she whispered, "It started about two years ago. My father had passed away, and not long after, I had a big fallout with my in-laws. Things at home haven't been the same since. My marriage has felt... cold."

Her voice broke. She covered her face and cried silently, tears that had clearly been waiting years to fall.

That was the moment everything shifted for me.

Her fibromyalgia wasn't just a dysfunction of nerves or muscles. It was a message, her body's desperate attempt to be heard when her voice had been silenced. The pain wasn't psychosomatic in the way it's often dismissed but it was psycho-physiological, rooted in very real emotional injury.

Rita wasn't ill in the traditional sense. She was grieving. She was angry. She was exhausted not just physically, but emotionally and spiritually. Her body had become the stage where her untold story was playing out.

The Physiology of Emotion

Cases like Rita's are not isolated. They are numerous, often unseen, misinterpreted, or dismissed. They lie in the gray zone between traditional medicine and the realm of lived human experience. And as we now understand, they are not "all in the head", they are very much in the body.

Chronic stress, especially of the silent, internalized kind, triggers profound biological responses. The sympathetic nervous system, which prepares us for "fight or flight," becomes overactive. Cortisol, our primary stress hormone, floods the body. Initially adaptive, this chronic hormonal surge becomes destructive over time.

Cortisol dysregulation can:

- Suppress immune function, making the body prone to infections and inflammation.
- Disrupt sleep cycles, contributing to insomnia or non-restorative rest.
- Tighten muscles, especially around the neck, shoulders, and back regions commonly affected in fibromyalgia.
- Alter gut function, leading to digestive issues that further drain energy.
- Affect menstrual and reproductive hormones, disturbing the delicate hormonal balance in women.

In Rita's case, every one of these systems was impacted. Not because they were independently diseased, but because her entire internal world was locked in a defensive posture. Her body was protecting her the only way it knew, by bracing, tightening, and holding on.

This is not metaphorical poetry but it is measurable biology. The emerging fields of psychoneuroimmunology and epigenetics are now proving what ancient traditions have long known: our emotional life has a profound effect on our cellular life.

Healing Beyond Prescriptions

In Rita's case, the turning point didn't come from higher doses of medications or stronger muscle relaxants. It came from acknowledgement. From holding space. From listening.

I referred her to a compassionate counselor. I suggested journaling as a tool for her to reconnect with her voice, one that had been buried beneath roles, expectations, and unresolved grief. We incorporated homoeopathy and Bach flower remedies, not as cures, but as allies in her emotional recalibration. And most importantly, I created an atmosphere in our consultations where she felt safe enough to be seen not just as a patient, but as a person.

Over the next six months, her transformation was gradual but undeniable. The pain didn't vanish overnight, but it became manageable. Her periods normalized. Her eyes regained some sparkle. And one day, she smiled a quiet, radiant smile that said more than any test result ever could.

What changed wasn't just her body. It was her relationship with herself. The act of being heard had given her permission to heal.

Medicine Needs a Broader Lens

Rita's journey became my wake-up call. I began seeing more cases where the real pathology wasn't just in the organs but in the stories we hadn't been trained to listen for. The woman with recurrent migraines who was silently enduring an emotionally abusive marriage. The man with chronic eczema who had never grieved his child's loss. The teenager with IBS whose anxiety was screaming for attention through his gut.

Modern medicine is brilliant in many ways, particularly in acute care and surgical interventions. But when it comes to chronic illnesses, especially those that defy lab reports, we often fall short. We reduce people to symptoms. We chase numbers. We treat the visible and ignore the invisible.

As doctors, we are taught to fix. But healing, I've learned, often begins with *feeling*. With listening. With presence.

We need to evolve from being mere diagnosticians to being compassionate witnesses.

The Invitation

This book is an invitation to doctors, to patients, and to anyone who has ever felt unseen in their suffering.

To doctors: let us not forget that behind every pathology lies a person. The most powerful diagnostic tool we have is not the latest machine, it's our presence, our ability to truly listen.

To patients: you are not broken. You are not imagining your pain. Your body is not betraying you but it is protecting you. It speaks the language of symptoms when words are not enough.

To all readers: healing is not a destination, but a homecoming. A return to the self, to safety, to truth. And it starts with acknowledgement.

Rita changed my practice but more than that, she changed me.

She reminded me that true healing requires more than science. It requires a soul.

The Invisible Thread – Mind and Body Are One

"The doctor treats, but nature heals." – Hippocrates.

This profound quote captures the subtle yet powerful truth that underpins all of healing: the body knows how to heal itself when supported in the right way. There is a saying in medicine that resonates deeply with this. "Treat the disease, and you might win. Treat the person, and you will always heal something." These words did not fully land for me until years into my clinical practice, when repeated encounters with patients showed me the limits of purely physical interventions.

In the formative years of my medical journey, my focus mirrored my conventional way of practice—treat the body, correct the numbers, and prescribe appropriately. But over time, an uneasy pattern emerged. Many patients who followed every instruction, took every pill, and adhered to every protocol still remained stuck in their illness. It wasn't the science that was failing, it was that something vital was being overlooked. Something invisible, something no investigation could measure: the inner world of the patient, their mind, their emotional history, their unseen wounds.

One such case was Neela, a 38-year-old homemaker who walked into my clinic with chronic pelvic pain and irregular bleeding. She had a long trail of investigations and consultations behind her. From hormone panels to ultrasounds, nothing pointed conclusively to why her suffering persisted. What her file didn't say, however, was what her weary eyes and deflated voice revealed: she was emotionally exhausted. It wasn't until I asked her a simple, compassionate question, "Are you under any personal stress?", and that the truth began to unfold. Her pain was not just physical. It was the echo of a life where she felt invisible, unheard, and emotionally starved.

That encounter with Neela was a turning point. Her uterus, a symbol of feminine identity and power, was holding decades of repression and emotional pain. Her condition wasn't merely gynecological, it was symbolic. From then on, our approach shifted. It wasn't just about medicines anymore. It was about helping her reclaim her sense of self-worth, her voice, and her identity. And as she reconnected with herself, her body slowly followed.

What began as anecdotal experience found scientific validation when I delved into the emerging field of psychoneuroimmunology. This discipline illustrates how our thoughts and emotions directly influence immune function and hormonal balance. Chronic stress, for instance, leads to excessive cortisol production—a hormone that can suppress immune function, heighten inflammation, and derail digestion. Emotional trauma has now been conclusively linked with autoimmune diseases like lupus and rheumatoid arthritis, gut disturbances such as IBS, hormonal imbalances including PCOS and thyroid disorders, and chronic conditions like fatigue syndrome.

Each emotion we feel has a biological echo. Fear contracts blood vessels. Anger elevates blood pressure. Grief suppresses immune response. Chronic worry disrupts gut flora. Guilt, when carried long-term, interferes with cellular repair and regeneration. These are not metaphors, they are measurable changes, rooted in our biology. This is where the wisdom of ancient traditions converges with modern science.

Beliefs, too, mold our biology. The placebo effect is perhaps the most celebrated example of mind over matter, where belief in healing produces real, measurable changes. Conversely, the nocebo effect shows how negative expectations can exacerbate illness. I will discuss these in a separate chapter. A diagnosis delivered without hope can act like a curse, increasing symptoms and despair. This isn't magic but it's the power of belief pathways in the brain triggering hormonal and immune responses.

This is why I now see the body not as a faulty machine but as a wise messenger. Every symptom is a signal, a form of communication. A migraine might be asking for rest. A skin eruption might signal emotional suppression. Chronic fatigue could be a result of prolonged emotional labor. Lower back pain might reflect an internal sense of unsupported burden. When we only silence these signals with medications, we rob ourselves of understanding the deeper call for healing.

One of the most touching things a patient ever said to me was, "Doctor, I feel like you see all of me, not just my disease." That, to me, was the essence of healing. To be seen, to be heard, and to be acknowledged as a whole human being. This realization redefined my practice. I no longer chase symptoms. I pursue stories. I listen not just with my ears, but with presence, with empathy, and with the understanding that every chronic disease might be rooted in an emotional truth.

Looking back, I often wonder how many patients I may have missed, patients whose minds were pleading for attention while I was focused only on their blood tests and scan reports. But I've learned that it's never too late to begin again. The moment we open the door to emotional inquiry, we shift the landscape of healing. We bring into the room a medicine that is intuitive, human, and enduring.

The mind and body are not two entities joined by coincidence. They are one seamless system, constantly communicating. You cannot heal one without touching the other. And when you begin to treat both, the visible and the invisible, you initiate a transformation that is truly holistic.

Coming up next....

In the next chapter, we'll explore a phenomenon that connects nearly every chronic condition I've encountered is **stress.** Often silent, often misunderstood, it is the modern epidemic silently shaping the landscape of disease. Let us go deeper.

CHAPTER III

The Stress Trap – Modern Medicine's Blind Spot

"It's not the load that breaks you down, it's the way you carry it." – Lena Horne

For a long time in my medical practice, I believed stress was just a background noise in the story of chronic disease, an afterthought rather than a central character. Like many physicians, I would end consultations with a polite reminder: "Try to relax, don't take tension." It was well-meaning but insufficient advice. With experience, I came to realize that this view was not only incomplete but it was dangerously misleading.

Stress is not a minor factor in chronic illness. It is often the spark that ignites the fire and the fuel that keeps it burning. Despite the tremendous strides modern medicine has made in treating physical symptoms, managing blood sugar, controlling blood pressure, reducing inflammation, we rarely pause to ask: *What is driving this disease from beneath the surface?* Again and again, the quiet but persistent answer is: **stress**.

The Undefinable Disease

Stress is elusive. It doesn't show up in routine blood work. There's no scan that highlights its presence. And yet, its fingerprints are found across nearly every system in the human body. It weakens the immune system, disrupts hormonal balance, disturbs sleep, slows digestion, and suppresses the body's natural capacity to heal.

In clinical practice, I began to recognize a recurring pattern. Patients who were "stuck" in their recovery despite accurate diagnoses and evidence-based treatments, often shared one common denominator: unresolved, chronic stress. They weren't just fighting disease. They were trapped in survival.

A Common Pattern Among Chronic Patients

Consider the case of Kiranbhai, a 45-year-old businessman who visited my clinic with a cluster of complaints like high blood pressure, acidity, insomnia, and chronic neck stiffness. On the surface, his lifestyle seemed healthy and he maintained a reasonably balanced diet. But his body was tense, alert, restless, overworked.

In conversation, he revealed something telling: *"Doctor, I sleep with my phone on my chest. I'm scared to miss a client's call. I haven't taken a holiday in ten years. If I stop, everything will fall apart."*

That one sentence captured the essence of chronic stress. Kiranbhai's body wasn't diseased but it was exhausted from years of bracing for impact. He was always on guard, constantly anticipating the next threat, be it real or imagined. His nervous system was stuck in perpetual overdrive, locked in the physiological state we know as "fight or flight."

This hypervigilance where muscles remain tight, digestion is impaired, immunity weakens, and healing stalls, is the classic stress response. And over time, it lays the foundation for chronic illness.

Understanding the Stress Response

The stress response is deeply wired into our biology. When the brain perceives danger, whether from a physical threat like a tiger or a psychological one like a looming deadline, it activates the **sympathetic nervous system**. This releases stress hormones such as **cortisol**, **adrenaline**, and **noradrenaline**, triggering a cascade of changes:

- Heart rate increases
- Blood pressure rises
- Digestion slows or stops
- Immune function is suppressed
- The brain shifts into survival mode

This system is designed to be temporary, a life-saving mechanism to help us flee danger or fight back. But in modern life, this response is often activated not for minutes, but for months or even years. Chronic stress is no longer about running from wild animals. It's about running from expectations, deadlines, financial strain, social pressure, and self-imposed standards of perfection.

Modern Stress Is Silent but Dangerous

Unlike emotional traumas that scream for attention, modern stress whispers. It hides behind a polished façade. Overworking is praised. Sleep deprivation is seen as ambition. Constant busyness is mistaken for productivity. But while the outer world applauds our resilience, the inner body keeps count.

Unresolved stress can manifest as:

- Hypertension resistant to medications
- Recurrent skin issues with no identifiable trigger
- Chronic acidity, migraines, or fatigue
- Fertility challenges without clear cause
- Thyroid imbalances, especially in multitasking women

These are not isolated symptoms. They are the body's language and its way of asking for help, of signaling that it is out of alignment. Yet in conventional medical settings, we often fail to ask the most crucial question: **"What is this body trying to tell us?"**

Why Stress Remains a Blind Spot in Medicine

There are several reasons why stress remains under-recognized in medical practice:

- It does not appear in lab reports
- It lacks a definitive diagnostic code
- It requires time and deep listening
- It demands self-reflection from both patient and physician

In truth, stress challenges the very structure of mainstream medicine, which is fast-paced, protocol-driven, and focused on tangible results. But healing requires a slower, more holistic gaze. And that begins with awareness.

My Own Blind Spot as a Physician

I must admit that for years, I too overlooked the impact of stress in my patients. It wasn't due to negligence, but rather a limitation of time given to patients. Though homoeopathic Medical school teaches me to ask about emotional health, it was only through years of patient conversations, watching their expressions, noticing their breathing patterns, sensing the silence between their words, that I began to truly understand the weight they carried. I began to ask deeper questions:

- "When did these symptoms begin and what was happening in your life at that time?"
- "What worries you the most?"
- "How are your relationships?"
- "What keeps you awake at night?"

Time and again, the answers revealed emotional roots far deeper than any scan or test ever could.

The First Step to Healing: Awareness

Many patients believe that stress is an unavoidable part of modern life. And to a degree, that is true. But **chronic** stress, the kind that lingers day after day, is not natural. The body is built for resilience, but it is also built for recovery. What it is not built for is continuous alertness. That leads to burnout, breakdown, and eventually disease.

Healing begins with a shift in understanding:

- Slowing down is not laziness—it is wisdom
- Rest is not indulgence—it is medicine
- Emotions are not distractions—they are signals
- Healing the mind is not separate from healing the body—it is essential to it

In the Next Chapter...

Now that we've uncovered stress as a hidden but powerful contributor to chronic illness, we'll journey into the next frontier of healing—the **biology of belief**. We'll explore how thoughts, expectations, and subconscious programs influence not just emotions, but actual cellular biology. Because true healing isn't only about outer treatments, it is also about **inner transformation**.

CHAPTER IV

The Biology of Belief – How Thoughts Shape Our Health

"Whether you think you can, or you think you can't—you're right." – Henry Ford

There are moments in a doctor's journey that leave a permanent imprint, not just on the mind, but on the soul. I remember one such moment with a woman named Pritiben. She was 52 years old and had recently received a diagnosis that many fear: breast cancer. Her fear was palpable, her vulnerability open. But more striking than the diagnosis itself was the way she spoke about it. With quiet certainty, she said, "I knew this would happen. I always feared I would get cancer someday. It runs in my family. It was bound to come to me." Her words carried more than just fear; they echoed conviction, a deep-seated belief that illness was her fate.

In that moment, it struck me with unusual clarity: before cancer ever touched her physical body, it had already occupied her mental landscape. This wasn't superstition or mere coincidence, it was programming. A silent inheritance of thoughts and beliefs, passed down through generations or absorbed from the environment, influencing biology without us even realizing it. That day marked a turning point for me, as I began to understand with new depth what Bruce Lipton has spent years teaching: our beliefs do not merely shape our emotional world; they shape our **cellular** world.

Beliefs Live in the Body, Not Just the Mind

Conventionally, we think of beliefs as abstract, mental constructs, passive ideas floating in the realm of consciousness. But modern neuroscience and the field of epigenetics present a radical shift in this understanding. They reveal that our beliefs are not passive. They are active signals. They translate into chemical messages that travel throughout the body, influencing gene expression, immune responses, hormonal secretion, and even the pace at which we heal.

Imagine for a moment that your body is constantly eavesdropping on your thoughts. It listens when you say, "I'm not safe," "I am broken," or "I'll never get better." It listens when you fear, when you doubt, and when you despair. These thoughts generate emotions like fear, helplessness, sadness. Emotions, in turn, activate a cascade of biochemical changes: cortisol levels rise, immune markers drop, inflammation spikes. Over time, this internal climate created and sustained by belief becomes the soil in which either health or illness takes root.

This is not mysticism. It is cellular biology. It is the science of how mental signals become molecular events.

The Placebo and Nocebo Phenomena: Mind Over Molecules

The medical world has long acknowledged the **placebo effect**—where a sugar pill, devoid of active ingredients, can bring about real healing simply because the patient believes in its power. This phenomenon, once considered a nuisance in clinical trials, has now become a window into the incredible power of belief. But equally potent though far less discussed is its darker counterpart: the **nocebo effect**. When a person expects a negative outcome, when they fear that a treatment won't work or believe that their condition is hopeless, their body aligns with that expectation. Symptoms may worsen, responses to genuine medication may diminish, and healing may stall, not because of the physical illness, but because of the mind's deep programming.

In my practice, I have seen both unfold. Patients who embraced a randomly chosen homoeopathic remedy with faith and optimism experienced profound improvement. Others, receiving the best constitutional remedy with deep case taking, spiraled downward, not for lack of medicine, but for lack of belief. They were drowning in doubt, in fear, in silent surrender.

Beliefs: Inherited, Absorbed, Installed

One of the most revealing insights I've gained is that many of our beliefs are not even truly our own. They are inherited like heirlooms. From parents who say, "Heart disease runs in our family." From society, which whispers, "Once you turn fifty, your health declines." From medical diagnoses that impose lifelong labels as, "This is chronic. You'll have to manage it forever."

Such beliefs lodge themselves deep in our subconscious, functioning like background apps in a smartphone. Invisible, yet always running. They shape how we perceive our symptoms, how we relate to our body, how we respond to illness, and ultimately, how long and how well we live.

A Case of Healing Beyond the X-Ray

Let me share a story that continues to inspire me. Rameshbhai, a retired schoolteacher in his 60s, came to me with advanced osteoarthritis. He struggled to walk, lived in constant pain, and had been told firmly that surgery was his only hope. But when we began to talk, I quickly realized that his suffering extended beyond his joints. Since retirement, he had begun to feel irrelevant. "I am of no use now," he confessed. This belief that he had outlived his value was as heavy as any physical ailment.

Our work together went beyond cartilage and ligaments. We explored identity, purpose, and belief. Slowly, we rewrote his internal story. He began meditating, moving with joy instead of fear, and mentoring students once again. His gait improved. His pain reduced. The X-rays didn't show drastic change but Rameshbhai had changed. His biology had shifted not because of a miracle, but because of a meaningful change in his mental environment.

The Science of Dr. Bruce Lipton: Cells Are Listening

The teachings of Dr. Bruce Lipton, a pioneering cell biologist, profoundly reshaped my perspective. In his landmark book *The Biology of Belief*, Lipton explains how cells respond not merely to genes but to their environment and crucially, to **the environment shaped by our thoughts**. His research showed that when identical stem cells are placed in different petri dish environments, they become different types of cells—muscle, bone, or fat—depending on what they're exposed to. If cells behave this way outside the body, why wouldn't they behave similarly inside?

This leads to a paradigm shift: **genes may load the gun, but it is the environment and our beliefs that pull the**

trigger. We are not passive victims of our DNA. We are active co-creators of our health.

Words as Medicine: The Power of the Doctor's Belief

As doctors, our words carry more weight than we often realize. A single sentence can seed hope or despair. If I say, "This is incurable," I may have unintentionally planted a nocebo. But if I say, "With the right support, your body can heal," I may ignite belief, perhaps the most powerful medicine of all. Over the years, I've become acutely aware of this responsibility. Every diagnosis is a suggestion. Every prognosis is a prophecy. And every word we speak has the power to heal or to harm.

Rewriting the Inner Script

So how do we begin to reverse the impact of damaging beliefs? The first step is **awareness**. We must encourage our patients and ourselves to ask reflective questions: *What do I believe about my illness? What story am I telling myself about my body? Where did that story come from? Is it even true?*

Often, people begin to see that their internal dialogue is soaked in fear and limitation. Once identified, this script can be rewritten, not overnight, but with conscious intention. Through affirmations, therapy, mindfulness, and even gentle spiritual practice, we can begin to rewire belief systems. And as the mind changes, so does the body. This is the very essence of psychoneuroimmunology, the science of how thoughts influence immunity and health.

A Message to You, the Reader

If you are reading this chapter while facing a chronic condition, let me offer you something beyond statistics or prescriptions. Let me offer you **a belief**, one that your cells are waiting to hear:

Your body is listening. Your healing is not only possible, it is already beginning the moment you choose to believe. Your first medicine is your mindset. Every thought is a signal. Every belief is a blueprint. And within you lies the extraordinary power to shape your biology with belief.

Coming Up Next: In the next chapter, we will delve deeper into the emotional roots of illness which are those hidden wounds, repressed memories, and unspoken sorrows that often take shape as physical symptoms. Because sometimes, the body speaks when the heart can no longer hold the silence.

CHAPTER V

When the Heart Speaks Through the Body – Emotions as Messengers

"The body keeps the score." – Bessel van der Kolk

There is a lesson I had learned earlier in my medical journey which is taught throughout our homeopathic training and now whispered through lived experiences and unspoken stories: the body is not merely a mechanical system that breaks; it is an intelligent organism that speaks. And when it speaks, more often than not, it is speaking the language of the heart.

In my early years of medical practice, I approached symptoms with a strictly biomedical lens. A headache was categorized under migraines or tension types. A gastric ulcer was attributed to H. pylori or hyperacidity. Back pain? Likely a disc bulge, postural strain, or muscular inflammation. It was a clean, logical, and systematic way to interpret disease, orderly and rooted in diagnosis. But despite all this knowledge, a deeper mystery lingered: why did some patients heal so quickly, while others with identical diagnosis remained stuck in cycles of chronic illness?

The missing link began to emerge in quiet consultation rooms, during moments when patients shared something unexpected, something not physical, but emotional. I started to recall my training as our teachers explained the role of mind as described in a book *"organon of medicine"* by Dr Samuel Hahnemann— founder and father of homoeopathy. These stories became doorways to understanding that illness is not just dysfunction; it is often a form of expression. A language used by the psyche when the soul can no longer hold its pain in silence.

I remember a woman named Mina, aged 39, who came to me with recurring rashes that no dermatological treatment seemed to cure. Steroid creams brought temporary relief, but the eruptions kept returning, more angrier, more redder, more defiant each time. On our third visit, driven more by instinct than protocol, I asked her softly, "Is there anything stressful going on in your life?" Her eyes filled instantly, and her voice dropped to a whisper. "Doctor," she said, "I've been silently enduring emotional neglect in my marriage for years. I haven't cried in front of anyone. I feel like I'm burning from the inside."

That sentence froze time for me. *Burning from the inside.* It wasn't metaphorical, it was diagnostic. Her skin wasn't merely reacting to allergens or autoimmune triggers. It was expressing the unexpressed. It was crying out where her words had failed. From that day, I stopped viewing symptoms as mere problems to be fixed. I began seeing them as messengers, sometimes loud, sometimes subtle, but always meaningful.

Modern psychosomatic research now affirms what ancient healing systems like Ayurveda and Traditional Chinese Medicine have emphasized for centuries: emotions, when unacknowledged, do not disappear. They embed themselves into the tissues, the cells, the nervous system. Grief finds refuge in the lungs, explaining why loss often brings breathlessness. Suppressed anger can lodge in the liver and gallbladder. Fear often settles into the kidneys, impacting hormonal balance and vitality. Chronic sadness can strain the heart, and persistent worry disrupts the gut, disturbing digestion and nutrient absorption.

The case of Ravi, a 28-year-old man with irritable bowel syndrome, offers another glimpse into this silent dialogue between mind and body. He had endured every GI test imaginable, endoscopies, diet regimens, medications, yet his gut remained in turmoil. As we revisited his life history, a detail surfaced: his father had passed away suddenly when he was just 15. In a matter of days, he had gone from being a child to becoming "the man of the house." He held himself together stoically, never fully mourning the loss. That grief, swallowed whole, found its expression years later, not in tears, but in cramps, bloating, and gut distress. His gut was weeping the tears his eyes never could.

As I treated more such patients, I began to see an emotional map underlying chronic disease patterns. Throat issues often linked with the inability to express truth. Chronic fatigue signaled emotional exhaustion, a soul carrying too much responsibility for too long. Autoimmune disorders, intriguingly, often revealed patterns of internalized self-judgment where the body, confused by emotional scripts of "not enough," turned against itself. Hormonal imbalances in women frequently reflected unresolved wounds around identity, femininity, and worth.

This does not mean every physical illness has a psychological cause, nor does it invalidate the role of viruses, genetics, and environmental toxins. Rather, it invites us to expand our lens. To understand that the body is not just a battleground, it is a canvas where the inner world paints its story.

Symptoms, then, become sacred. They are not nuisances to be silenced, but messengers to be understood. And healing, in many cases, is not just about prescribing the right medicine, but about asking the right question: *What is the soul trying to say through this suffering?*

This perspective has changed my practice, not just as a doctor, but as a human being. I've started listening with a different kind of stethoscope. Not just to heartbeats and bowel sounds, but to the tremors of unspoken pain, the cadence of suppressed emotion, the rhythms of silent heartbreak. Often, all it takes is a question delivered with empathy: *"What were you going through emotionally when this started?"* More often than not, the answers hold the key.

To my fellow doctors, I offer this reflection: medicine must not only be the science of the body, but it must also be the art of listening to the heart. Because when we fail to ask about emotional pain, we may be missing half the diagnosis.

And to you, dear reader, if you're carrying a chronic illness, I invite you to sit quietly with your symptoms. Not with fear, but with curiosity. Ask your body: *What are you trying to tell me that I have been unwilling to feel?* Perhaps there is an emotion you locked away years ago. Perhaps there is a truth you've never dared to speak. Perhaps there is grief you never gave yourself permission to grieve.

This is not about blame. It is about listening with compassion. Because healing doesn't always come from doing more. Sometimes it comes from finally feeling what we never allowed ourselves to feel.

Coming Up Next....

In the next chapter, we will begin exploring practical tools and emotional release techniques. Its gentle yet powerful ways to help patients, and even we as doctors, move from pain to freedom, from suppression to expression. Because once we recognize the body's language, the next step is to respond, not with more medication, but with deeper understanding and presence.

CHAPTER VI

Emotional Detox – Releasing What the Body Carries

"You've got to feel it to heal it."

There exists a silent burden that many patients carry, not something visible on their skin or evident in their blood reports, but something deeply embedded within the very tissues of their being. These are the burdens of **unfelt emotions**, **uncried tears**, and **unspoken truths**. They do not show up on MRIs or X-rays. They cannot be captured in a lab test. And yet, they exert a powerful influence on a person's health, vitality, and ability to heal.

Modern medicine is adept at treating the physical symptoms. Antibiotics for infections, anti-inflammatories for pain, antihistamines for allergies. But what about the emotional residue left unaddressed? What about the silent storms people have weathered for years without ever naming them? Just as the body accumulates physical toxins from food, environment, and lifestyle, it also accumulates **emotional toxins** from trauma, stress, heartbreak, betrayal, neglect, and unexpressed grief.

This chapter is a journey into that invisible realm, the world of emotional detox. It's about creating the space, permission, and safety to **release what the body has been holding onto for far too long.**

A Case That Astonished Me

Some cases leave a mark on a doctor's soul, not because of their complexity, but because of the depth of human experience they reveal.

Neelam was in her early forties when she came to me. She suffered from **fibromyalgia**, a chronic condition marked by widespread musculoskeletal pain, fatigue, and sleep disturbances. For her, the pain wasn't just physical; it was existential. She described it with words that still echo in my memory: *"It's a pain I carry everywhere."*

We tried every conventional approach. Prescription medications, dietary shifts, physical therapy, nutritional supplements. She was co-operative and committed, yet the improvements were minimal and temporary. Something deeper was going on.

One day, almost instinctively, I asked her a question that changed the direction of her healing: **"If your body could speak, what would it say?"**

She fell silent. Then, she replied in a slow tone. Her answer was simple, raw, and transformative: *"It would say... I'm tired of pretending I'm okay. I've been the strong one for everyone, my parents, my husband, my children. I never complained. But I've been lonely for years."*

In that moment, the room shifted. This wasn't just about fibromyalgia anymore. Her body had been a container for years of **emotional suppression**, of being the silent caregiver, the invisible warrior, the one who carried everyone else without asking for support.

Her tears didn't just flow, they **released** something. That day marked the beginning of her true healing. Not from a pill. But from finally acknowledging what had been locked away for too long.

What Is Emotional Detox?

Emotional detox refers to the **intentional process of identifying, feeling, and safely expressing suppressed emotions**. It is as crucial as detoxifying the liver or gut, yet often more neglected.

It is not about "fixing" your emotions.It's about **freeing** them. Freeing *yourself*.

Here's what emotional detox entails:

- **Recognizing** emotional patterns that have been buried or denied.
- **Allowing** those emotions to rise to the surface without judgment.
- **Releasing** them through safe, embodied, and compassionate expression.

People often ask, "Isn't it dangerous to open up old wounds?"

My answer: "It's more dangerous to let them fester."

Why Do We Suppress Emotions?

From a young age, society trains us to **deny, minimize, or avoid** our emotional experiences.

- *"Don't cry like a baby."*
- *"Anger is bad—be polite."*
- *"Don't question authority and respect your elders."*
- *"Stay strong. Don't show weakness."*

These teachings, though often well-intended, cultivate emotional repression. We learn that certain feelings, especially sadness, rage, grief, or fear are unacceptable. So we tuck them away. But these emotions don't disappear. They **go inward** into the muscles, the fascia, the joints, the gut, the immune system. They become cellular memories.

The body becomes a **warehouse of emotional leftovers**. And over time, that warehouse gets heavy. Symptoms arise. Sometimes subtle, sometimes severe. But always with a story beneath them.

How the Body Releases

The body is not just a machine; it is an **emotional organism** with its own language for healing.

When we allow ourselves to feel, the body begins to discharge stored tension and trauma in powerful, often surprising ways:

- **Tears**: Emotional tears are rich in stress hormones. They are the body's most ancient form of detox.
- **Shaking or trembling**: Seen in wild animals after trauma, this is the body's way of discharging survival stress.
- **Crying, yawning, sighing, sweating**: All signs that the nervous system is shifting from "fight-or-flight" to "rest-and-release."

I have witnessed patients who cried deeply after decades of holding it in and their migraines reduced. Others screamed into pillows or journaled honestly for the first time in years and their eczema began to heal. Some faced long-avoided truths and their IBS symptoms calmed.

Emotional expression is not a luxury. It's **medicine**.

Safe Ways to Detox Emotionally

Here are **doctor-approved, research-informed**, and **personally validated** ways to support your emotional detox:

1. Journaling Without Censorship

Take out a notebook and write **exactly** what you feel, not what you think you *should* feel. No filters. No edits.

Prompt: *"What am I angry, sad, or anxious about that I haven't admitted yet?"*

This form of raw expression allows hidden emotions to surface, often revealing what lies at the root of physical distress.

This is my favourite technique to release emotional toxins.

2. Speaking the Unspeakable

Sometimes, the deepest healing happens when we finally say what we've been too afraid to speak.

Speak it in therapy. Speak it in prayer. Speak it to the mirror. Or write it in a letter never meant to be sent.

Expression is freedom.

3. Crying Without Guilt

Crying is not a sign of weakness. It is a natural, intelligent form of emotional release.

Many patients instinctively apologize when they cry in my clinic. I gently stop them and say: *"Please don't apologize. This is medicine too."*

4. Movement for Emotion

Our emotions are stored not just in the mind but in the **body**. Movement can unlock and move these energies.

Try:

- Intuitive dancing

- Shaking exercises
- Yoga
- Walking in nature

Let your body lead. It knows the way.

5. Therapeutic Touch or Bodywork

Therapies like **massage, craniosacral therapy, acupuncture, or Reiki** can help release emotional tension stored in deep tissue layers.

Touch, when offered safely and skillfully, can bypass the mind and communicate directly with the body's wisdom.

6. Talking to the Body

This may sound unusual, but it's profoundly effective.

Speak to your body with compassion. Try saying: *"Dear body, I'm here. I'm ready to listen. You can let go now. Thank you for carrying me."*

Sometimes, all the body needs is **acknowledgment**.

A Doctor's Reflection

Does emotional detox cure all diseases? No. But it can:

- **Accelerate healing**
- **Lighten symptoms**
- **Prevent relapses**
- **Restore emotional balance and hope**

There are times when **no amount of medication** can do what a single emotional breakthrough can. As a doctor, I have learned to create safe spaces, not just for diagnosis and prescriptions but for **truth, expression**, and **release**.

If You Are Carrying Emotional Weight...

Let me say this to you from the heart: You are **not broken**. You are **full**.

Full of memories, unmet needs, moments that never got a voice. And now, your body is gently asking for space to be heard, to be seen, to be unburdened.

Healing begins when we listen.
When we allow the body to tell its story.
When we feel what we were never allowed to feel.
When we release what no longer needs to be carried.

Coming Up Next...

In the next chapter, we will explore how to build **emotional resilience** through powerful mind-body tools like **breathwork, meditation, guided imagery**, and more. Because healing is not only about what we release but also about what we **nurture within**.

CHAPTER VII

Mind-Body Medicine – Practices That Promote Inner Healing

"You can't calm the storm. So stop trying. What you can do is calm yourself. The storm will pass."

As a doctor, we treat the physical body, organs, tissues, symptoms, and lab values. Our medical education is steeped in diagnostics, prescriptions, and procedures. We are taught to ask the right questions, prescribe the right drugs, and follow the protocol. The mind? That was often relegated to psychiatrists or psychologists, not general practitioners like myself. But thanks to the Homoeopathic system of medicine, which considers the totality of symptoms giving more weightage to the mental symptoms and patterns.

Though I knew theoretically, It took me years through both personal struggles and clinical experience to arrive at a simple yet profound realization: **the mind is not separate from the body.** It is, in fact, the operating system. Just as a computer cannot function properly if its software is glitchy or overloaded, the body cannot heal fully if the mind is anxious, fearful, or constantly in survival mode.

We cannot truly heal the body without addressing the mind. This chapter explores that intersection, that sacred meeting point between medicine and mindfulness. It is not about replacing traditional medicine. It is about complementing it and creating space where healing isn't just about eliminating disease, but about restoring inner balance.

The Science of Mind-Body Healing

What we think and feel is not merely "in our head." Thoughts are biochemical signals. Emotions have physical consequences. The mind speaks to the body through hormones, neurotransmitters, and subtle energy currents. Modern research in neuroscience, immunology, and psychoneuroendocrinology affirms what ancient healing systems always knew: **the body responds to the mind.**

Consider these well-documented findings:

- **Meditation** lowers cortisol, the primary stress hormone, and has been shown to reduce systemic inflammation.
- **Breathwork** activates the parasympathetic nervous system, shifting us out of the fight-or-flight state and into rest-and-digest mode.
- **Visualization** enhances immune markers, and in some studies, even accelerates recovery after surgery.
- **Gratitude** increases levels of dopamine and serotonin—neurochemicals associated with happiness, resilience, and immunity.
- **Simple human touch**, intentional silence, and loving awareness can elevate oxytocin, reduce pain, and promote healing.

In essence, **how we feel emotionally determines how we heal physically.** Chronic stress, repressed emotions, and negative thought patterns can sabotage even the best medical treatments. But inner calm, clarity, and emotional connection can accelerate healing in ways that science is only beginning to understand.

Patient Story: From Panic to Peace

Amrutbhai, a 52-year-old businessman, came to me with a dual diagnosis: **hypertension and recurring panic attacks**. He was on medication, and while his blood pressure was somewhat under control, he lived with constant fear of traffic, crowds, elevators, even sudden phone calls. His mind was a battlefield, and his body was caught in the crossfire.

On one particularly anxious day, I gently introduced him to a simple breathing technique. He was skeptical, perhaps even slightly embarrassed. But within a week, I saw a visible shift, his shoulders dropped, his face softened, and his breath slowed.

"Doctor... this feels different," he whispered.

We created a simple plan: **five minutes of breathwork, twice daily.** Within three weeks, his panic attacks had reduced by 80%. His blood pressure stabilized. He started taking the stairs again, smiling more freely, and even began enjoying public spaces. The transformation wasn't dramatic but it was **real, sustainable, and profound.**

That day I understood something deep: **sometimes the most powerful prescription isn't written on paper but it's practiced in silence.**

Mind-Body Practices That Heal

Here are the practices I now teach my patients and use personally. They are simple, free, accessible to all, and profoundly effective.

1. Breathwork – The Bridge Between Mind and Body
The breath is a direct portal to the nervous system. It's always with us, yet often overlooked. Conscious breathing

allows us to shift our inner state in real-time.

Technique: 4-7-8 Breathing

- Inhale through the nose for 4 seconds
- Hold for 7 seconds
- Exhale slowly through the mouth for 8 seconds
- Repeat for 4–5 cycles

Benefits: Reduces anxiety, lowers blood pressure, improves sleep, calms the vagus nerve, and creates immediate relaxation.

2. Mindful Meditation – Coming Home to the Moment

You don't need to be spiritual or sit cross-legged in the Himalayas. Just sit with yourself.

How to Start:

- Sit quietly with eyes closed
- Focus on the breath
- When thoughts come (they will), gently return to the breath
- No judgment. Just presence.

It's also known as **ANAPANA**

Benefits: Reduces inflammation, increases gray matter in the brain, enhances focus, and promotes emotional regulation.

3. Body Scan – Releasing Stored Tension

Our body stores unprocessed emotions often as tightness, fatigue, or unexplained discomfort.

Practice:

- Lie down comfortably
- Bring your awareness from feet to head, slowly

- At each body part, notice any tension
- Say mentally, "Relax"

This simple practice reconnects you with your body's innate wisdom and can significantly improve sleep quality.

4. Guided Imagery – Healing Through Imagination

The brain does not differentiate between imagined and real experiences. Use this to your healing advantage.

Visualize:

- A golden light entering your body
- A white wave cleansing your organs
- Your heart softening
- Your cells glowing with health

Regular imagery has been shown to reduce pain, speed healing, and empower patients facing chronic conditions.

5. Gratitude Journaling – Changing Your Chemistry

Gratitude is not just a virtue, it's a biochemical upgrade. **Try this nightly:**

- List 3 things you're grateful for
- One thing you did well today
- One person you appreciate

This practice rewires neural pathways, boosts mood-regulating neurotransmitters, and strengthens emotional immunity.

6. Vipassana- your internal journey

Vipassana isn't the scope of this book. You can't learn it theoretically. You have to experience it. Try out if possible in any vipassana center which is located all over the globe.

"But Doctor, Will This Really Help My Disease?"

Let's be honest and grounded.

No, breathwork will not cure cancer.

No, meditation won't reverse diabetes overnight.

No, visualization won't replace necessary medication or surgery.

But here is the truth:

These practices **reduce the internal chaos** that often worsens disease. They enhance the **receptivity** of the body to medical treatment. They **reduce side effects**, promote emotional strength, and create a space where **healing becomes possible, not just physically, but emotionally and spiritually.**

They don't replace medicine. **They empower it.**

As a Doctor and a Patient

There was a time in my life when I, too, was burning the candle at both ends. Sleepless nights, endless responsibilities, the emotional toll of caregiving—it all added up. My body started sending signals: fatigue, acidity, headaches. I ignored them. Like many doctors, I thought self-care was optional.

Until I couldn't ignore them anymore.

It was through breathwork, mindful pauses, and reconnection with my own inner world that I began to heal, not just physically, but as a human being. And that's when my practice changed. My approach shifted from purely treating symptoms to **supporting the person as a whole.**

Your Mind Is Medicine

You don't need to be perfect. You don't need to be spiritual. You just need to be **willing**—willing to pause, to breathe, to feel.

Because your body is listening. It's not your enemy. It's not broken. It's waiting for **you** to return.

And healing begins the moment we stop fighting ourselves and start **supporting our wholeness.**

Coming Up Next...

In the next chapter, we explore how belief systems and subconscious programming silently shape our healing journey. What you believe about your illness, your body, and your identity, whether you realize it or not, creates a powerful blueprint for how your biology responds.

Because the body listens not only to medicine...**But also to the mind's deepest truth.**

CHAPTER VIII

Belief is Biology – The Power of the Subconscious in Healing

"Whether you think you can, or you think you can't, you're right." – Henry Ford

In chapter 4, we have explored Biology of Belief. Now we will understand that Belief is Biology.

In the conventional medical schools it is taught that healing was a biochemical process, an interplay of medications, diagnostics, surgeries, and numbers on a lab report. My early perception of medicine was shaped by evidence-based protocols and pharmacological interventions. But as the years went by, experience started to tell a different story, one that could not always be explained by science alone. I began noticing a recurring phenomenon: two patients with the same diagnosis, receiving the same standard of care, often had drastically different outcomes. One would respond swiftly to treatment, moving toward recovery, while the other, despite identical interventions, would struggle, relapse, or remain unwell.

This inconsistency prompted a deeper inquiry. What was different between these patients? Often, it wasn't something tangible like their medical history or physiological markers. The difference lay in something far more subtle but profound, their **belief systems**. It was in the way they perceived their illness, the internal dialogue they carried, and the silent script playing continuously in the background of their subconscious mind. That's when I began exploring a fascinating intersection between modern neuroscience and ancient wisdom: the idea that our beliefs, particularly those held subconsciously, have the power to shape our biology.

The Subconscious: Your Inner Operating System

We like to think we are rational beings, consciously steering the course of our lives. But research in neuroscience and psychology tells a different story. It is now widely accepted that 90 to 95 percent of our actions, decisions, emotions, habits, and even physiological responses are governed not by our conscious thoughts, but by our subconscious mind. This subconscious functions like an invisible operating system quietly yet powerfully running the scripts that dictate how we experience the world.

These scripts are often written early in life. They're shaped by childhood conditioning, cultural norms, religious beliefs, personal experiences, traumas, and the repeated thoughts we've internalized over time. These beliefs can become embedded so deeply that they operate automatically, often without our awareness. And many of them are limiting in nature. Beliefs such as *"I always get sick in the winter," "My illness is genetic, I'm powerless to change it,"* or *"I don't deserve to be healthy"* become not just mental ideas but biological instructions. The body listens and responds. These beliefs influence everything from immune function and hormone levels to nervous system regulation and cellular repair.

Patient Story: Healing by Changing the Script

Let me tell you about Heenaben, a 47-year-old woman who had been suffering from chronic migraines for over 15 years. She had seen multiple specialists, undergone countless tests, all of which came back normal, and tried every medication imaginable. The results were always temporary; nothing brought lasting relief. When she came to me, she was exhausted not just physically, but emotionally and spiritually.

Instead of diving into another battery of tests, I asked her a question she hadn't heard before: *"What do you believe these migraines are trying to say to you?"*

She looked startled, perhaps even a bit skeptical. But after a long, reflective silence, she responded: *"It's the only time I allow myself to stop. To rest. To be taken care of."*

That moment was a turning point. Together, we uncovered a core belief rooted deep in her childhood: *"To be loved, I have to suffer or sacrifice something."* This subconscious narrative had been playing in the background for decades. Her body had become the canvas on which this belief was expressed. Over the course of several weeks, we worked on that belief. Along with medication I also suggest tools like journaling, mindfulness, conscious affirmations, and gentle self-inquiry.

Her migraines didn't disappear overnight, but they began to soften. The frequency is reduced. The severity diminished. Eventually, they stopped. Heenaben's biology followed her belief.

The Origins of Belief

So where do these powerful beliefs come from? Most are inherited, not genetically, but psychologically. We absorb them through childhood messages, such as *"Don't play in the rain, you'll get sick,"* or *"Illness is punishment from above."* We internalize cultural or religious ideologies that glorify suffering or discourage questioning authority. We see patterns in our families, illnesses passed down from generation to generation and unconsciously assume the same fate for ourselves. And most powerfully, trauma implants beliefs that we are broken, unworthy, or doomed to struggle.

Over time, these beliefs calcify. They operate silently, outside of our conscious awareness, yet they shape how our bodies function, heal, and age.

Changing the Script: Practical Tools for Healing

As a doctor, I've learned that shifting a belief system is not about delivering a motivational speech or handing over a list of affirmations. It requires gentle, sustained awareness and a willingness to look inward. Here are some of the tools I use with patients, and even in my own life:

1. Identify the Core Belief

Begin by asking reflective questions:

- *What do I believe about my illness or body?*
- *What did I learn about health growing up?*
- *Do I truly believe healing is possible for me?*

Journaling is one of the most effective ways to bring these subconscious scripts into conscious awareness. It allows the hidden stories to surface.

2. Challenge and Replace

Once a core belief is identified, the next step is to gently challenge it. Ask: *Is this really true? Has this belief served me?* Then begin the process of conscious replacement. For instance, instead of *"My body always betrays me,"* say: *"My body is doing its best to protect me. I'm learning to understand its language."*

Repeat these new affirmations daily, write them down, say them out loud, and most importantly, feel them. Emotions are the glue that seals a belief into the subconscious.

3. Visualization

The subconscious mind doesn't distinguish between reality and vividly imagined experience. Use this to your advantage. Visualize yourself not as someone hoping to heal, but as someone already healed. Feel it. See it. Experience it in your mind's eye. This mental rehearsal sends signals to the brain, which adjusts your body's chemistry accordingly.

What I Now Know as a Doctor

There are moments in clinical practice when I pause, look a patient in the eyes, and say:

"You're not broken. You've just been carrying beliefs that no longer serve you. Let's rewrite them together."

And more often than not, that moment more than any prescription becomes the catalyst for true healing.

A Question for You

If you're reading this chapter, I invite you to reflect:

- What beliefs have you carried about your body until now?

- Have those beliefs helped you or harmed you?
- Are you willing to try on a new belief, even if just for today?

You don't have to believe in magic. Just believe in *possibility*. That shift alone creates new neural pathways, balances hormones, soothes the nervous system, and enhances immune response. That's biology. And that's healing.

Coming Up Next...

In the following chapter, we'll explore how chronic stress and unresolved trauma affect the nervous system and immune health. We'll dive into the science of dysregulation and discuss how creating internal safety can be the missing link in chronic disease recovery. Because it's not just about what you eat or what you take, It's about how safe your body feels to *heal*.

CHAPTER IX

The Nervous System – Where Safety Unlocks Healing

"The body will not heal in survival mode. First, it needs to feel safe."

For many years in my clinical practice, I approached chronic illness through the lens of physical symptoms. I treated pain with analgesics, fatigue with tonics, acidity with antacids, allergies with antihistamines, and even autoimmune diseases with immune suppressants or modulators. Some patients improved. Many didn't. And I began to notice something that medicine rarely talked about: the patients who struggled the most to heal were often those who felt unsafe, not just physically, but emotionally, relationally, and even spiritually.

This wasn't a coincidence. These patients weren't more diseased or less compliant. Rather, their bodies were stuck in a state where healing wasn't even on the table. Their physiology was operating as if the world were dangerous and unpredictable. The common thread? Their nervous systems were trapped in a loop of survival. And that state, while incredibly useful for acute threats, makes chronic healing virtually impossible.

The Nervous System: The Body's Inner Control Tower

The autonomic nervous system, which governs the functions of our internal organs without conscious effort, has two major branches: the **sympathetic nervous system (SNS)** and the **parasympathetic nervous system (PNS)**. The sympathetic system activates the classic "fight or flight" response. It's our evolutionary defense mechanism, meant to respond to real and present danger. In contrast, the parasympathetic system facilitates "rest, digest, and heal." It's the state our body needs to enter for cellular repair, digestion, immune regulation, and hormonal balance.

Both branches are necessary. They're meant to work in harmony. However, in the landscape of chronic disease, especially in today's high-stress, overstimulated environment, many patients are stuck in a sympathetic overdrive. This is not the dramatic panic state one might imagine, but a more insidious low-level hyperarousal like an alarm that never fully turns off.

In this state, the body deprioritizes healing. Why would it heal when it believes it's being chased by danger? Trying to heal in such a condition is like trying to repair an airplane mid-flight during turbulence. The basic maintenance cannot begin until the plane has landed safely.

A Patient's Story: Reema and the Survival Loop

Reema was a young woman who came to me with severe ulcerative colitis. Her symptoms waxed and waned, but there was a curious pattern, her flare-ups always worsened when her husband left town for work. Her gut, it turned out, was not reacting to food allergens or microbial imbalances. It was reacting to fear. Reema lived in a near-constant anticipatory state: "What if I fall sick again?" "What if I can't take care of the kids alone?" "What if something goes wrong while he's away?"

Her body wasn't malfunctioning; it was responding to perceived threat. We tried dietary changes, medications, probiotics but nothing made a lasting difference. It wasn't until we began focusing on her **nervous system regulation** that a real shift occurred. She started practicing grounding techniques, gentle breathwork and journaling. Three months later, her flares decreased significantly, her digestion stabilized, and her energy returned. More than that her eyes had a sparkle I hadn't seen before. Safety had returned to her system, and her body responded with healing.

What Chronic Stress Does to the Body

Chronic stress doesn't just affect the mind. It's a full-body event. A nervous system stuck in survival mode causes an array of downstream effects:

- **Suppressed immune function**, making one prone to infections and inflammation.
- **Elevated cortisol levels**, which disturb the delicate hormonal balance and increase systemic inflammation.
- **Poor digestion and nutrient absorption**, due to blood being shunted away from the gastrointestinal tract.
- **Muscular tension and chronic pain**, as the body stays braced for impact.
- **Sleep disturbances**, because the brain cannot shift into restorative modes.
- **Emotional numbness or hyper-reactivity**, as the brain learns to anticipate threats even when none exists.

Worse, the brain adapts to this hypervigilance, normalizing the stress response and making it harder to recognize peace even when it's present. This is the tragic irony that healing becomes biologically impossible not due to the disease itself, but because the body believes it cannot yet afford to heal.

The Vagus Nerve: A Highway to Healing

At the center of the parasympathetic system lies the **vagus nerve**, an extraordinary cranial nerve that connects the brain to the lungs, heart, gut, and even kidneys. The vagus nerve plays a pivotal role in calming the body, reducing inflammation, improving digestion, and regulating mood.

When the vagus nerve is **toned and active**, the parasympathetic system can do its job: promote homeostasis and healing. Fortunately, we don't need complicated interventions to stimulate the vagus nerve. Simple, natural practices can be profoundly effective:

- **Humming or chanting** (especially mantras like OM).
- **Cold exposure**, such as splashing cold water on the face or finishing a shower with cool water.
- **Deep diaphragmatic breathing**, where the belly rises more than the chest.
- **Gentle yoga and movement**, to release muscular bracing.
- **Authentic emotional expression**, including laughter and tears, both of which discharge stored emotional energy.
- **Singing**, especially from the diaphragm.

I often tell my patients, "If you can hum, breathe, or smile, you've already begun your healing journey."

Daily Practices for Nervous System Regulation

Nervous system healing doesn't require hours of effort. In fact, it thrives in simplicity and consistency. Here are three practices I commonly prescribe:

1. The 5-5-5 Grounding Technique

Take a moment to pause. Name:

- 5 things you can see,
- 5 things you can hear,

- 5 things you can physically feel (your clothes, the chair, the air on your skin).

This practice anchors awareness into the present moment, pulling the brain away from future anxiety or past rumination.

2. Coherent Breathing

Breathe in for 5 seconds, out for 5 seconds, and repeat for 5 minutes.

This rhythmic breathing entrains the heart and nervous system into coherence. This is a balanced state that promotes healing across multiple systems.

3. Safe Touch and Self-Soothing

Place one hand gently on your chest, the other on your belly. Feel the rise and fall of your breath. Whisper to yourself, "I am safe now."

It might feel awkward initially, but with repetition, this gesture becomes a powerful signal to your nervous system that the emergency has passed.

What I've Learned as a Doctor

Over the years, I've come to a sobering conclusion: **no medication, no supplement, no surgery can replace a regulated nervous system.** I've witnessed patients doing everything "right", eating organic foods, taking prescribed medication, practicing yoga, yet remaining sick. It wasn't until they addressed their nervous system dysregulation that the needle moved. It turns out, healing isn't always about doing more. Sometimes, it's about doing less with greater awareness and gentleness.

Your Body Is Not Broken—It's Just Stuck

If you've been ill for a long time, you may have begun to feel betrayed by your body. But perhaps what feels like betrayal is actually protection. Your nervous system is not flawed. It is overprotective because it was taught to survive, not to trust. It has learned to live in defense mode, anticipating danger. The way forward is not through fighting your body but by befriending it. Offer it consistent messages of safety. Show it that the danger is over. The body will follow.

True healing begins when the body feels safe enough to stop surviving and start thriving.

Coming Up Next...

In the next chapter, we will explore the hidden burden of **emotional suppression and unprocessed grief** in chronic illness. Because emotions that are buried alive don't die, they take up residence in the body. And sometimes, the first step toward recovery is not a pill or a protocol, but a single tear finally allowed to fall.

CHAPTER X

The Body Keeps the Score – Emotions, Trauma, and Disease

Our bodies are not just mechanical structures composed of muscles, organs, and bones. They are living journals. Every unspoken word, every swallowed emotion, every buried trauma, they inscribe their story deep beneath the skin, weaving themselves into the tissues, often unbeknownst to us. Over time, these unexpressed experiences do not simply vanish. Instead, they wait, simmering quietly until they manifest through the language of physical symptoms.

I recall a moment from my practice that I will never forget. Harsh, a middle-aged man, had been suffering from chronic back pain for almost seven years. His diagnostic reports were consistently normal. Painkillers offered him only fleeting relief. When he visited my clinic, he sat across from me with a tired, almost defeated smile and said, "I guess this is just my cross to bear." Yet something within me urged me to dig deeper. I gently asked, "Tell me... what was happening in your life around the time this pain first began?" His eyes shifted away, and silence enveloped the room. Slowly, in a broken tone, he revealed, "That was the year I lost my father... I had to hold everything together for the family. I never even had time to cry." At that moment, it became crystal clear, his back was bearing more than physical weight; it was carrying years of unexpressed grief.

In conventional medicine, we are trained to observe the body mechanistically, as a system of parts and processes. But true healing demands a shift in perception. We must learn to view the body as a living, breathing diary, a dynamic storehouse of experiences, memories, and most importantly, emotions. Unfelt grief, unspoken anger, unresolved fear, these do not simply disappear. When there is no safe place to express them, the body becomes their keeper. They embed themselves in muscles, tissues, and even organs, silently waiting until one day they are forced into expression through chronic disease.

Scientific research is finally catching up to what ancient healing traditions have long understood: the body keeps the score. Studies have demonstrated that suppressed emotions activate the sympathetic nervous system, locking the body into a chronic state of fight-or-flight. Over time, this unrelenting stress response disrupts immune function, increases systemic inflammation, and disturbs hormonal balance, which is setting the stage for disease. Research has consistently shown that individuals with unresolved childhood trauma face significantly higher risks for a host of chronic illnesses, ranging from cardiovascular diseases and autoimmune disorders to chronic fatigue, irritable bowel syndrome (IBS), and even certain forms of cancer. Dr. Bessel van der Kolk's seminal work, **The Body Keeps the Score**, masterfully elucidates how trauma is not merely a psychological event but a physiological one, reshaping the body's biology unless actively processed and released.

I encountered another profound example with a patient named Jyoti, a 35-year-old woman struggling with autoimmune thyroid disease. She had been on standard medications for years, yet her symptoms like profound fatigue, anxiety, hair loss, and mood disturbances persisted stubbornly. She appeared to be the quintessential "strong one," always smiling, always composed, never complaining. However, when I broached the subject of emotional stress, a fragile vulnerability emerged. She whispered, "I had two miscarriages back-to-back. I never cried. I just kept moving." In truth, it wasn't merely her thyroid that was inflamed but it was her unexpressed grief and heartbreak. Her body had been crying out for her. With support, Jyoti began to process her grief through therapy, journaling, and gentle emotional expression. Over time, her blood markers improved, her energy returned, and her anxiety lessened, not because of a new drug, but because she had finally allowed herself to feel what she had long buried.

Nearly two decades of medical practice, I began noticing recurring patterns that could not be dismissed. Patients with repressed anger often struggled with hypertension, gastrointestinal acidity, and liver dysfunctions. Those harboring deep, unprocessed grief frequently presented with lung-related conditions, persistent breathlessness, or profound depressive symptoms. Individuals with porous emotional boundaries were disproportionately represented among those with autoimmune conditions as if the body's immune system mirrored the individual's inability to defend emotional boundaries. Fearful, anxious patients often reported a spectrum of gut-related disturbances, from IBS to chronic indigestion, sometimes accompanied by full-blown panic disorders. Although these patterns are not diagnostic in themselves, they were too consistent to ignore. Intriguingly, when these patients began to address their suppressed emotions, through therapy, bodywork, or expressive practices, many experienced remarkable improvements in their physical health.

The question then arises: **How do we release these stored emotions from the body?** Healing requires conscious, daily practices that invite suppressed feelings into awareness.

One powerful tool is **emotional journaling**. Each evening, I encourage patients to reflect: *What emotion did I avoid today? What did I wish to express but held back? Where do I feel tension in my body right now?* By writing without filters, we allow the body's unsaid stories to surface onto the page, providing catharsis and insight.

Another vital practice is **safe emotional expression.** Emotions are energy in motion, they need to move. Cry if the tears come. Scream into a pillow if rage rises. Punch a cushion. Laugh without restraint. Dance until the emotions have space to release. The body is not concerned with the form, it simply needs an outlet.

And above all, **seeking therapy is not a weakness, it is wisdom.** Just as we refer patients to a cardiologist without hesitation, we must normalize referrals to skilled therapists when emotional healing is essential to physical recovery. Integrating mental health support into holistic medical care is no longer optional; it is imperative.

I am not a master in all therapies described in this book. But I have read them and even practiced them sometimes. And not all the patients whom I recommend these therapies are responsive to it. Most of the patients are not willing to do it or abandon the technique in between. The examples of patients given in this book are merely 1 % of patients to whom I recommend therapies. They believe in the process and get benefits.

After years of practice, this much I know: Healing does not occur solely through prescriptions and procedures. True healing occurs in granting ourselves and others 'permission'.

Permission to feel.

Permission to express.

Permission to grieve.

Permission to forgive.

Permission to finally let go.

No symptom is purely physical. Often, it is the body's final cry for acknowledgment, for a chance to speak when words have failed. The body keeps the score until we are ready and willing to listen.

If you are reading these words, perhaps your body too has been carrying silent burdens. I invite you to ask yourself:

What emotions have I buried deep inside? What am I afraid to feel?

Can I allow myself to express without judgment?

You do not have to resolve everything at once. Healing is not an event; it is a journey. Begin simply by feeling, one *feeling* fully today. Trust that when you do, the body– ever wise, ever patient– will begin the work of restoration.

Coming Up Next...

In the next chapter, we delve into the fascinating world of the gut-brain connection; exploring how your emotions, your nervous system, and your gut microbiome are in constant, intricate conversation. We will uncover how this three-way partnership influences not just your digestion, but your immune system, mental health, and susceptibility to inflammation. Because, as you will discover, what you feel... is exactly what your gut feels too.

CHAPTER XI

The Second Brain – How the Gut Feels Your Emotions

We often say, "I have a gut feeling about this," almost casually, as if it's just a figure of speech. Yet, what if that instinct was more than metaphorical? What if your gut was truly sensing your emotions, sometimes even before your conscious mind fully registers them?

In my years of treating patients with chronic illnesses, especially those involving digestive disorders, a curious pattern emerged. Two patients, both diagnosed with irritable bowel syndrome (IBS), were prescribed identical medications and placed on the same carefully structured diet. Yet, while one would recover remarkably, the other continued to struggle.

What separated them?

The difference often lay beyond physiology and pharmaceuticals. It lay in the emotional realm. The patient who improved had begun addressing their internal emotional landscape, working through layers of stress, grief, or suppressed anger. Meanwhile, the patient who remained unwell was still carrying, and often suppressing, emotional turmoil.

This observation led me into the fascinating scientific frontier now known as the **Gut-Brain Axis**, a powerful, two-way communication system that intertwines our emotions and our digestion at a fundamental biological level.

Your Gut: More Than Just a Digestive Organ

The gut is astonishingly complex. It houses over **100 million neurons**, more than the spinal cord itself, earning it the nickname "**the second brain.**" It is not a passive organ waiting for instructions; it actively communicates with the brain, sending emotional and physical feedback constantly.

Even more astonishing, the gut is responsible for producing **95% of the body's serotonin**, the neurotransmitter most closely associated with feelings of happiness and well-being. Other neurotransmitters like dopamine and GABA, crucial for mood regulation, are also significantly influenced by gut activity.

This intricate dialogue between the gut and the brain explains why:

- Your stomach clenches with anxiety.
- Digestion slows when you're feeling depressed.
- You experience instant gut reactions during moments of anger or fear.
- Diarrhoea in children during or before examination.

In essence, while the brain *thinks* your thoughts, the gut *feels* them. It is a visceral, immediate, embodied emotional response system. And it often senses danger, unease, or joy far more quickly than rational thought processes can.

The Vicious Cycle: How Stress Damages the Gut (and Vice Versa)

Under stress, your body shifts into **sympathetic nervous system dominance**, the classic "fight or flight" response. Blood is shunted away from the digestive organs toward the muscles and brain to prepare for survival action. In this stressed state:

- Digestive secretions reduce.
- The gut lining becomes more permeable (a phenomenon sometimes called "leaky gut").
- Beneficial gut bacteria die off, while harmful strains proliferate.
- Inflammation spreads throughout the gut and body.

The result? Digestive symptoms like bloating, cramping, constipation, diarrhea, acidity, and overwhelming fatigue. But this isn't a one-way street.

The distressed gut, in turn, sends signals back up the vagus nerve to the brain, exacerbating feelings of anxiety, depression, brain fog, and irritability. This creates a **feedback loop** where the mind and body continually reinforce each other's distress, making healing difficult unless the cycle is intentionally interrupted.

I often look for psychological intervention in a patient with GI disturbance without pathological causes.

Swati's Story: Healing the Mind to Heal the Gut

One patient who profoundly illustrated this connection was Swati, a vibrant 29-year-old woman battling persistent gastritis and IBS. Despite trying an extensive range of treatments, probiotics, antacids, gluten-free diets, Ayurvedic herbs, her symptoms persisted, leaving her frustrated and fatigued.

In our consultation, I asked her a simple but critical question: *"When did your symptoms begin?"*

She hesitated, then admitted quietly, "*After my divorce. I tried to pretend I was fine, smiling for the world... but inside, I was falling apart.*"

Recognizing the deep emotional wound behind her physical symptoms, we embarked on a dual healing journey in association with homoeopathic medication:

- **Emotional Support:** Journaling therapy, and honest emotional expression helped her to process the pain she had buried.
- **Nervous System Regulation:** We incorporated daily breathwork, gentle gut massage, and grounding practices to bring her autonomic nervous system back toward safety and balance.

Within two months, her gut symptoms began to dissolve, *not* because of only a magical medicine, but because she created a safe, nurturing internal environment where her body could finally let go of chronic stress and inflammation.

The Microbiome: Your Invisible Emotional Ally

Another critical piece of the gut-emotion puzzle lies in the microbiome—the bustling community of trillions of bacteria living symbiotically within us.

Far from being passive inhabitants, these microbes:

- Help digest complex carbohydrates and fibers.
- Train and modulate our immune system.
- Synthesize essential vitamins.

- Influence mood by producing neurotransmitters and modulating inflammation.

Under chronic stress, however, the microbiome falls into a state of **dysbiosis**, where beneficial bacteria decline and pathogenic bacteria overgrow. Dysbiosis contributes to:

- Increased gut permeability.
- Widespread inflammation.
- Mood disorders like anxiety and depression.
- Poor immune responses.
- Skin issues, hormonal imbalances, and sleep disturbances.

When your gut microbiome is unbalanced, it is not just digestion that suffers, it touches nearly every aspect of your physical and emotional health.

Practical Gut-Healing Tools from My Clinic

Healing the gut requires more than supplements or diets; it requires creating an environment, both internal and external, where safety, relaxation, and nourishment are prioritized. Some practical interventions I recommend include:

1. **Eat in Peace:**
   Meals are sacred. Avoid eating with distractions like TV, smartphones, complaining or arguments. Allow mealtimes to be moments of mindfulness, where your body feels safe enough to digest.
2. **Bitters Before Meals:**
   A slice of lemon, a piece of fresh ginger, or a few drops

of a digestive tincture before eating can prime your digestive system naturally, enhancing enzyme secretion and bile flow.

3. **Breath Before You Bite:**
   Pause for three slow, conscious breaths before meals. This simple ritual activates the parasympathetic "rest and digest" system, improving both nutrient absorption and digestive efficiency.

4. **Gut Massage and Touch:**
   Gentle, clockwise abdominal massage stimulates the vagus nerve, promotes bowel movement, and signals the body that it is safe.

5. **Probiotics and Fermented Foods:**
   Incorporate naturally fermented foods like yogurt, buttermilk (chaas), and homemade pickles (in moderation) to nourish and diversify your gut flora.

Yet, remember: even the best nutrition cannot heal a gut that remains tense, fearful, or disconnected from emotional truth.

A Shift in Philosophy: Safety First, Then Healing

Earlier in my career, I believed that if I could fix the gut through medications, supplements, or diets, the patient's emotional and mental state would improve naturally. Now, experience has taught me a deeper truth: When a patient feels truly *safe*, physically, emotionally, and relationally, the gut begins to heal itself.

The gut is not just a digestive organ. It is an emotional antenna, a barometer of inner safety, and sometimes, your very first cry for help.

A Gentle Invitation

If you are struggling with gut issues, I invite you to ask yourself:

- When do my symptoms tend to flare up?
- What emotions might I be holding tightly in my belly?
- Can I offer myself compassion and patience instead of judgment?

And perhaps whisper this affirmation to your body:

"Dear gut, I am listening now. You are safe to soften. You are safe to heal."

Coming Up Next...

In the next chapter, we will explore the surprising reality of the **placebo and nocebo effects**–how your beliefs can profoundly alter biology itself. Because sometimes, what you believe about healing can be even more powerful than what you do.

CHAPTER XII

The Power of Belief – Placebo, Nocebo, and Mind-Driven Medicine

"What the mind believes, the body begins to become."

One afternoon, a patient walked into my clinic with a spark in her eyes that no lab report could measure. She was diagnosed with polymyalgia rheumatica, an invisible storm of symptoms: chronic fatigue, body-wide pain, broken sleep, emotional exhaustion. On paper, her case was complicated, messy. Her biochemical markers suggested a long, uphill journey. She was suggested to consult me by a relative of hers who had benefited from my treatment. When she spoke, her voice carried a quiet certainty.

"Doctor," she said, smiling, "I just know I will get better."

At first, I nodded politely, thinking of the long management protocols ahead. But within three months, this woman was walking briskly, returning to her work, laughing without hesitation. No miracle drug had been introduced. No radical new therapy had been given. What, then, had fueled her turnaround? Her mind had believed, with a kind of clarity and commitment, in her own recovery and her body had listened.

On the other hand, there are patients who come to me with relatively milder illnesses, yet when they glance at their reports, a shadow crosses their face. "I don't think I can ever heal," they whisper.

Their recovery often drags, plateaus, or remains incomplete not because their body is incapable, but because their mind has decided otherwise.

This deepened my fascination with the true power of belief in healing, what we medically label as the **placebo effect** and its

lesser-discussed opposite, the **nocebo effect**. Not as mere psychological curiosities, but as real, biological phenomena demonstrating how profoundly human consciousness can shape physiology.,

What Is the Placebo Effect, Really?

In clinical research, a placebo refers to an inert treatment, often a sugar pill, given to some participants to objectively compare it against an active drug. However, something astonishing happens repeatedly in these trials: patients who receive the placebo often show real improvement. They report less pain, reduced symptoms, better sleep, and even measurable changes in brain activity and hormonal patterns.

Why does this happen? Because belief itself triggers biological healing pathways. When a patient expects relief, the brain begins to release cascades of beneficial chemicals:

- **Endorphins**, the body's natural painkillers, flood the system.
- **Dopamine** surges, enhancing motivation and reward circuits.
- **Oxytocin** is released, fostering a sense of trust and connection.
- **Serotonin** rises, supporting mood stability and physiological balance.

In essence, the expectation of healing becomes a biochemical instruction, commanding the body to mobilize its internal pharmacy toward repair.

The Dark Twin: Nocebo Effect

But belief cuts both ways. If a positive expectation can heal, a negative expectation can harm. This phenomenon is known as the **nocebo effect**.

Patients who believe a medication will have side effects often manifest those exact symptoms even when given a placebo. Individuals who are told that their disease is incurable may subconsciously accept decline as inevitable, accelerating their deterioration. I have witnessed this countless times: patients burdened by grim medical forecasts ("There's no cure," "It'll only get worse") often fulfill those prophecies, not solely due to the disease itself, but because their belief system orchestrates a state of ongoing physiological stress, inflammation, and collapse.

The nocebo effect teaches us an urgent lesson: **words can wound just as powerfully as knives.** Every prognosis, every explanation, carries the risk of planting either seeds of healing or seeds of hopelessness.

The Brain: Not the Healer, But the Switch

It is critical to understand that the brain itself is not the *source* of healing but it is the **switchboard operator**. Every thought, belief, and expectation signals the nervous system to choose between two biological states:

- **Repair mode** (rest, recovery, healing)
- **Defense mode** (stress, inflammation, protection)

When a patient believes they are healing, the body shifts toward repair. When they fear worsening or despair, the body tightens into defense.

Importantly, **belief is not blind positivity.** It is not mere "positive thinking." True healing belief arises from:

- An internal conviction that life is trustworthy
- A readiness to receive restoration
- A safe emotional environment that calms survival instincts

A Patient Story: From Nocebo to Placebo

Amit, a 42-year-old man, arrived at my clinic carrying the heavy burden of a rare autoimmune skin disorder called Lupus Erythematosus. He had visited five different dermatologists, each of whom had given him the same discouraging prognosis: "This condition is permanent. It will keep flaring for the rest of your life."

Every month, as if on schedule, his skin erupted in painful rashes. The pattern was almost mechanical, an external reflection of an internal acceptance of defeat. He believed what he had been told: he was broken.

When Amit met me, I did not offer false promises. Instead, I said something different: *"Your body is confused, not broken. And confusion can be corrected."*

That single sentence lit a spark of hope. Through a combination of homoeopathic remedies, emotional coaching, and simple language shifts, Amit began to heal:

- He stopped referring to his body as "damaged."
- He stopped owning the disease as "mine."

- He started affirming: *"I am learning to heal."*

Gradually, his flare-ups became less frequent. His skin cleared. His posture straightened. His spirit lightened. His belief in his body's ability to heal had been rekindled and so the body responded accordingly.

Words as Medicine – Or Poison

In my early medical years, I thought clinical accuracy was enough. But now I realize: the words we speak to our patients are far more than information. They are **emotional prescriptions**.

To tell someone "You are incurable" is to inject despair into their bloodstream. To dismiss symptoms as "just anxiety" is to amplify their suffering through invalidation. Every careless phrase can become a hidden nocebo.

Instead, the doctor's language must become a bridge to safety and possibility:

- "Your body is intelligent. We will listen and learn from it."
- "Healing is possible. Let's take one step at a time."
- "Your symptoms carry meaning. We will honor and understand them."

The body listens to the mind and the mind listens to the words.

How to Activate Healing Belief – For Patients and Ourselves

Healing belief is not a fantasy. It can be cultivated, nurtured, and strengthened like a muscle. Here are some approaches I use with my patients and in my own life:

1. Create an Environment of Hope

Authentic hope is not denial of reality; it is the quiet assurance that possibilities exist beyond present pain. Safety signals to the nervous system: *"You are allowed to heal now."*

2. Rewrite the Inner Dialogue

I ask patients: "What are you saying to your body daily?" Is it criticism or compassion? Language creates biology. Speaking to oneself as a caretaker rather than a critic lays the foundation for cellular repair.

3. Rituals of Trust

Daily rituals, however small, anchor belief. Whether it's a morning walk, brewing herbal tea, prayer, meditation, or simply touching the heart and saying *"I am healing"*; these acts reassure the subconscious mind that healing is already underway.

4. Visualization

The subconscious does not distinguish vividly imagined experiences from reality. Guiding patients to *see* themselves active, joyful, and free of illness primes their biology toward that future.

My Deepest Realization as a Doctor

If there is one lesson the placebo and nocebo effects have taught me, it is this:

It is not always the strength of the medicine that determines recovery.

It is not always the stage of the disease that dictates prognosis.

It is not even the precision of treatment plans that moves the needle.

It is the **energy of belief**, the silent, often invisible current running underneath every biological process.

The placebo is not a trick or a lie. It is the living proof that the mind is not separate from the body, but its most potent ally. The nocebo is not a curse. It is a solemn reminder to never, ever strip away a patient's hope. **For hope itself is medicine.**

If You Are Reading This...

I invite you to ask yourself, gently:

- What do I truly believe about my illness or my healing journey?
- Do I believe I am worthy and capable of recovery?
- Can I shift from fear to curiosity, curiosity about what is possible for me?

And perhaps you might whisper to yourself today:
"My body wants to heal. My mind is ready to believe. I trust the process unfolding within me."

Coming Up Next...

In the next chapter, we will dive deeper into the power of **intention and visualization**, not merely as mental techniques, but as active tools to reprogram the body's internal chemistry and healing responses. Because the images you hold inside your mind begin to shape the reality you live outside.

CHAPTER XIII

Seeing is Believing – Visualization, Intention, and Cellular Change

"The body follows the blueprint held in the mind."

As a doctor, I have come to learn that healing is not just about medicines, lab reports, or clinical protocols, it is also about inner vision.

Sunita, a 38-year-old homemaker battling the relentless grip of **rheumatoid arthritis**. When she came to see me, her body was stiff, her gait hesitant, her joints swollen and inflamed. But what caught my attention even more than her physical pain was something in her eyes; a certain dimness, a loss of light, as if her spirit was too tired to hope.

After going through her history and reviewing her medications, I paused and gently asked her something unusual: **"Sunita, how do you see yourself five years from now?"**

Her eyes welled up instantly. She looked down and whispered, "Doctor, I don't. I can't see beyond the pain."

That moment struck me deeply. Here was a woman whose inner vision had collapsed. She could no longer imagine herself walking without pain, playing with her children, hugging her future grandchildren, or even doing everyday tasks with ease. Her body was not just struggling with disease but her *mind had forgotten how to picture health*. And if one cannot visualize a future without suffering, how can the body ever move toward it?

From that moment on, I began introducing something profoundly simple, yet incredibly powerful, into my consultations: **guided visualization** and **intentional imagination.**

What is Visualization, Really?

Let's be clear, visualization is not wishful thinking. It is not fantasy or denial of reality.
It is a **focused, intentional, conscious practice** of mentally rehearsing a desired state so vividly, so emotionally, that the brain begins to interpret it as real.

Modern neuroscience backs this up. When you **imagine walking**, the motor cortex, the part of your brain responsible for movement, activates just as it does when you actually walk. In other words, the brain doesn't distinguish much between **real experience** and **vividly imagined experience**. Visualization, therefore, **primes the nervous system**, training it to expect and accept a new reality.

More than that, it also sends signals deep into the autonomic nervous system, affecting immune function, hormone balance, blood pressure, and even gene expression.
When you imagine healing, your body begins to prepare for it.

Your Cells Respond to Mental Pictures

Every image you hold in your mind, conscious or subconscious, sends a biochemical message to your body. Thoughts are not just fleeting wisps of consciousness. They are **electrical impulses** that result in **chemical messengers** like neuropeptides, hormones, neurotransmitters, that travel through the bloodstream and **bind to receptors** on your cells.

This is not metaphorical. This is **molecular biology**.

When a person continuously thinks or imagines:

- **Hopelessness** → The body increases cortisol, the stress hormone, which suppresses immunity and accelerates inflammation.
- **Pain** → Neural pathways become hyper-sensitized; even small sensations become amplified.
- **Illness** → The immune system stays in constant alarm mode, leading to exhaustion and malfunction.

But when that same person begins to regularly imagine:

- **Recovery**
- **Calm and inner peace**
- **Joyful movement**
- **Strength and vitality**

...those thoughts **generate different signals**, and the cells respond in kind. Just as trauma imprints on the nervous system, **so can hope** but it must be consistent and emotionally anchored.

Dr jitendra Adhia, a renowned mind coach, has explained the concept of visualization in depth in his book ***VISUALIZATION.***

The Science of Intention

Closely related to visualization is **intention**, the active, emotional force behind our inner images.

Intention is not just a hope or a wish. It is **directed**

consciousness, fused with emotional energy and clarity. When intention is focused and repeated, it can affect the body in surprising ways.

Research in psychoneuroimmunology reveals that:

- **Focused intention** can modulate heart rate, immune responses, and even cellular repair mechanisms like DNA restoration.
- **Meditation and visualization** have been shown to lower inflammatory markers such as **interleukin-6 (IL-6)** and **C-reactive protein (CRP)**.
- Cancer patients who practice guided imagery often show **better treatment tolerance**, reduced side effects, and even improved outcomes.

And perhaps most remarkably, the **subconscious mind** which governs the majority of our physiological functions **does not distinguish between real and imagined input**. It responds to **emotion + repetition**. That is the secret ingredient.

Case Story: Healing Through Imagination

One of the most memorable transformations I've witnessed came from a patient named **Rajubhai**, a 55-year-old man with type 2 diabetes and worsening kidney function. His creatinine levels were climbing. Dialysis was being discussed. He came into my clinic with fear in his eyes and defeat in his shoulders. Instead of overwhelming him with lab values and prognosis, I offered him a different kind of prescription one that did not come in a pill bottle.

I asked him to practice a 10-minute daily visualization:

1. Sit comfortably.
2. Close his eyes.

3. Breathe slowly.
4. **Imagine your kidneys glowing** healthy, filtering gently, surrounded by warm healing light.
5. Feel gratitude as if the healing is already underway.

He was skeptical. But he trusted me and he tried.

Six weeks later, something remarkable had shifted. Not only did his lab parameters stabilize, but his energy had transformed. He stood taller. He smiled more. He even said he felt "lighter." No, his kidneys were not magically cured but he had stopped deteriorating. His inner vision had given his body **new instructions**.

A Simple Daily Visualization Practice

Today, I routinely share a short, structured visualization practice with many of my patients dealing with chronic conditions:

Morning Healing Visualization (5–10 Minutes)

- Sit or lie down in a peaceful spot.
- Close your eyes. Take three deep, calming breaths.
- Imagine your body surrounded by **a soft, warm, healing light**.
- Focus gently on the affected area whether it's the joints, the heart, the skin, or the gut.
- Visualize it:

  - Cooling inflammation
  - Regenerating healthy tissue
  - Flowing with vibrant circulation
  - Returning to natural balance

- Repeat a healing affirmation like: **"I am safe. I am healing. My body remembers how to thrive."**

Done daily, this becomes a **new inner script, one** that your cells begin to **memorize** and **act upon**.

From Doubt to Design

Healing is not merely the absence of disease. It is the **presence of inner order**, of clarity, of a body that remembers how to function in harmony. Visualization helps reawaken that memory. It bridges the gap between diagnosis and destiny.

Many patients come to me full of doubt. They ask, "Doctor, what if I can't heal?"

I now gently offer them a different question: **"What if your body is waiting for your mind to believe again?"**

That simple shift from fear to creative imagination can become the turning point.

As a Doctor, What I've Learned

In our practice we rarely **explore the patient's internal imagery**, how they see themselves, what they believe is possible, or what future they imagine.

Yet I have learned that these **inner pictures**, often unspoken, can be more powerful than any external intervention. The mind does not just interpret the world; it helps **create it**.

When we guide our patients to see healing, truly see it in their mind's eye, we invite them to **become co-creators in their recovery**. They are no longer passive recipients of treatment, but **active partners in transformation**.

If You're Reading This...

I invite you to pause and ask yourself:

- **What does my healed self look like?**
- **Can I imagine walking freely, breathing deeply, and smiling effortlessly?**
- **Can I create a few minutes of joy in my mind, even if only inside my imagination?**

Start with this simple affirmation:

"I see myself healing. I feel it. I trust it. My body is becoming it."

Repeat it. Live it. Breathe it. Because when you believe in your healing, you give your body **permission** to follow.

Coming Up Next...

In the next chapter, we'll journey deeper into the past. We'll explore how **trauma, emotional memory, and unresolved experiences** often shape patterns of chronic illness from the subconscious level. Because the mind does not forget and neither does the body.

CHAPTER XIV

The Body Remembers – Trauma, Memory, and Chronic Illness

"You may forget the pain, but your body never does, until it is heard."

In the quiet stillness of the consultation room, I have witnessed something remarkable, an unfolding that transcends charts, scans, and prescriptions. Patients often come to me for physical complaints: aching joints, relentless migraines, recurring allergies, irritable bowels, or inexplicable fatigue. Their language is clinical, their focus often strictly biological. But as I guide them through the story of their illness, probing gently into the timeline, listening between the symptoms, there often comes a pause. A still moment. Sometimes it's a sigh. Sometimes a subtle shift in posture. And then, quietly, the tears come. Not for the pain in the body, but for something much older and deeper, like abandonment, betrayal, heartbreak. A buried sorrow, long silenced, finally surfacing.

As a physician, I have come to understand something fundamental: **the body often carries what the heart could not bear**. When the mind is overwhelmed and cannot process certain emotional events, it is the body that remembers. It absorbs, stores, and sometimes cries out through chronic symptoms. Illness, then, is not always a breakdown; often, it is a message, like a coded expression of long-unacknowledged wounds.

Trauma is Not Just in the Mind

When people hear the word "trauma," they often think of war veterans, assault survivors, or victims of severe abuse. But trauma is far broader and more nuanced than these extreme examples. At its core, trauma is any event or series of experiences that overwhelm a person's capacity to cope, especially emotionally. What is traumatic is not only the event itself, but the internal experience of helplessness, fear, or abandonment it causes.

Trauma can manifest in many subtle and socially invisible forms. It might be a parent who never offered warmth or affection. A teacher who humiliated a child in front of peers. A partner who dismissed emotional needs or constantly criticized. Even sudden losses, a death, a job loss, a financial collapse or witnessing violence can imprint themselves deeply into the nervous system. These imprints are often unconscious and can remain hidden for decades, shaping behavior, perception, and most insidiously–physiology.

Crucially, childhood trauma, even when not overtly abusive, can lay the foundation for a lifetime of health challenges. This is because the young nervous system is exceptionally malleable and deeply attuned to emotional safety. Events we cannot even consciously recall such as prolonged parental absence, neglect, or emotional inconsistency, can shape how our body learns to respond to the world. Over time, **trauma unprocessed becomes tension embodied** and the body, in its wisdom, remembers.

The Biology of Suppressed Emotion

Science is increasingly validating what traditional healing systems have long asserted: unprocessed emotional trauma has profound biological effects. Chronic stress and emotional repression can dysregulate the autonomic nervous system which is the body's command center for survival and impair immune function, hormonal balance, digestion, and pain modulation.

Dr. Bessel van der Kolk, in his seminal book *The Body Keeps the Score*, provides compelling evidence that trauma doesn't just reside in memory, it physically alters the brain. The amygdala, our alarm center, becomes hyperactive, leaving us in a state of constant vigilance. The hippocampus, responsible for contextual memory, shrinks, leading to disorganized or suppressed recollections. The prefrontal cortex, essential for decision-making and emotional regulation, goes offline during stress, making us reactive or emotionally numb. This biological dysregulation becomes a chronic loop, predisposing individuals to inflammation, autoimmunity, and other chronic conditions.

Trauma, in essence, keeps the body locked in a state of defense even when the threat has long passed.

Case Study: The Grieving Gut

Reenaben, a 49-year-old woman, came to me after years of battling ulcerative colitis. Despite trying every conventional treatment, diets, steroids, immune modulators, her flare-ups persisted. She lived with exhaustion, frequent bleeding, and a sense of frustration. During one extended visit, in a rare moment of emotional safety, Reenaben spoke of her son who was killed in a car accident twelve years earlier. Since that day, she had not shed a single tear. She had buried the grief so deeply, she said, "If I let it out, I feel like I'll collapse."

That day marked the beginning of a different kind of treatment. Alongside her physical care, we began homoeopathic constitutional medication, somatic awareness, and guided emotional release. Over months, she slowly allowed herself to grieve. She cried for the first time since the funeral. As her emotional life reawakened, something profound happened, her gut began to heal. Flares reduced. Her energy returned. She began smiling again. Her colitis had, in truth, been her gut's cry for the grief her words could never express.

Emotions Are Chemical Events

Every emotion we experience generates a corresponding biochemical cascade. Joy releases serotonin and oxytocin. Anger triggers adrenaline and cortisol. Grief can lower immune markers, disrupt sleep, and impact cardiovascular health. When we suppress emotions, their neurochemical residue does not disappear, it finds new expression in the body.

- **Anger**, unspoken, may turn inward, fueling hypertension, acid reflux, or chronic muscular tension.
- **Fear** may hide in the gut, presenting as irritable bowel syndrome, panic attacks, or insomnia.
- **Grief** often settles in the lungs or heart space, manifesting as fatigue, breathlessness, or chest pain.
- **Shame**, perhaps the most corrosive emotion, can turn the immune system against itself, fueling autoimmune

disorders.

Symptoms, then, are not random errors but rather **messages** and expressions of emotional truths that have been buried too long. The body becomes the final storyteller when the soul has remained silent.

Signs That Trauma May Still Reside in the Body

While not always obvious, there are clues that past trauma may still be affecting physical health:

- Chronic pain or fatigue with no identifiable medical cause
- Heightened reactivity to minor stressors or conflict
- A sense of emotional numbness or disconnection
- Recurring illnesses that correlate with emotional triggers
- Feelings of being "stuck," both physically and mentally

Patients often describe a sense of alienation from themselves. "I feel like I'm living someone else's life." This is the nervous system trapped in a protective freeze, a state where safety has never fully returned.

Healing Trauma to Heal the Body

Healing is not about "going back" and relieving pain; it is about creating the conditions where safety and integration become possible. Here are approaches I've found both powerful and gentle:

1. **Safe Listening**
   Healing begins with being heard. When patients feel deeply seen and accepted, their nervous system can begin to relax. True listening without interruption, fixing, or judgment is the first medicine.

2. **Body Awareness**
   Helping patients become aware of bodily sensations not just symptoms, but areas of tension or numbness can restore the mind-body connection. Ask, "Where do you feel this in your body?" and "What does it feel like it wants to say?"

3. **Emotional Expression**
   Journaling, movement therapy, somatic therapies, and guided conversation can give voice to the unspoken. Homoeopathy, when skillfully used, can also support the safe release of long-held emotions.

4. **Nervous System Regulation**
   Breathing techniques, vagal nerve exercises, yoga, meditation, and touch therapy can help shift the body from sympathetic overdrive into parasympathetic healing mode.

5. **Forgiveness and Letting Go**
   Illness sometimes holds unprocessed anger or resentment like an identity. Releasing that through forgiveness, not as an obligation but as a liberation can unlock energy and vitality once thought lost.

A New Role for the Physician

In the evolving landscape of chronic illness, my role as a doctor has transformed. As stated in Organon of Medicine by Dr Samuel Hahnemann in aphorism 4, *"He is likewise a preserver of health if he knows the things that derange health and cause disease and how to remove them from persons in health"*. It prevents disease from taking the shape of chronic illness.

In a diseased person, I no longer focus only on when the symptoms began. I ask, "What was happening in your life before that?" I inquire, "When did you start carrying something alone?" Or, "When did you stop feeling safe in your own body?"

And when the story finally surfaces not just of disease, but of endurance, heartbreak, and silent strength, true healing can begin. Chronic illness is often not merely pathology, it is biography. It is the body's attempt to narrate what the person could not.

An Invitation to You, the Reader

If you are reading this, perhaps your body too has been holding on. I invite you to pause and ask:

- What pain have I quietly buried?
- What stories still live inside my cells?
- Can I begin to listen, without fear, without shame?

Then say softly to yourself:

"It's safe now. I can feel. I can heal. I can come home to myself."

Coming Up Next....

In the next chapter, we will explore the transformative power of mindful presence, how returning to the "now" can unravel old patterns, soothe the nervous system, and open the gateway to healing. Because ultimately, healing is not about fixing the past or fearing the future. It is about returning fully to the only place life exists: the present moment.

CHAPTER XV

Now is Where Healing Lives – The Power of Presence in Chronic Illness

"The mind lives in YESTERDAY and TOMORROW. But the body only lives in NOW."

Anilbhai, a 62-year-old businessman, had been struggling with chronic asthma for over a decade. Each time he sat in my consultation room, his words drifted far away from the present. "This all started after that awful business loss ten years ago," he'd say. Or, "If only I had done things differently back then..." Often, his thoughts would leap ahead into an uncertain future: "What if this condition worsens?" "What if I can't breathe during my next business trip?" Though his body was physically present in the chair before me, his mind was continuously caught in the gravitational pull of the past and the imagined catastrophes of the future. And so, despite medications and management, his healing seemed to remain distant and incomplete.

This experience with Anibhai is not rare. In fact, it reveals a central truth in the biology of healing: **the body can only heal in the present moment.** All the core functions that sustain life and repair disease like nervous system regulation, immune modulation, cellular regeneration, hormonal balance are operated in real time. They respond to what is happening *now*. However, when the mind is entrenched in past regrets or future fears, it triggers physiological states that mimic threat. The body, unable to differentiate between an actual danger and a remembered or anticipated one, reacts accordingly.

This has profound implications for those living with chronic illness. The nervous system, when exposed to repeated or sustained psychological stress, often rooted in mental time travel, enters a state of hypervigilance. It signals "unsafe" to the rest of the body. As a result, repair is postponed, inflammation is sustained, digestion is impaired, and sleep is disrupted. The body stays locked in survival mode. Chronic illness, therefore, does not simply live in the organs or systems but it lives in a nervous system that has forgotten how to feel safe. And the only place safety can be accessed is in the present.

When we practice presence, even for a brief period, we begin to offer the body a different message: "You are safe now." This simple but profound shift resets biological systems. Heart rate begins to slow. Cortisol levels, the stress hormone, begin to drop. Muscles, long held in tension, begin to release. Digestion improves as parasympathetic (rest-and-digest) activity is restored. Even brain waves shift from the frantic beta state of analytical thinking to the calmer alpha and theta states associated with creativity, relaxation, and healing.

This isn't abstract or philosophical. It is deeply rooted in science. Mindfulness-based interventions, tools that cultivate non-judgmental awareness of the present have consistently shown measurable outcomes in medical research. Inflammatory markers like IL-6 and TNF-alpha, often elevated in chronic disease, decrease. Patients with fibromyalgia, psoriasis, hypertension, and even cancer report improved quality of life, reduced symptoms, and decreased dependency on medications. Presence, then, isn't simply a nice idea. It's a **neurobiological imperative**.

I recall another patient, Rimaben, a 44-year-old schoolteacher who had been tormented by migraines for years. She had tried everything, medications, dietary changes, even alternative therapies. Still, her pain persisted. One day, instead of another new remedy, I offered her a new relationship with her pain. I invited her to try something very simple. "When the pain builds," I said, "pause. Don't resist. Don't label it as bad. Don't try to push it away. Just sit with it. Breathe. Witness." She agreed, skeptically, but began to practice a two-minute mindful observation technique whenever her migraine symptoms began to rise. Over time, something remarkable happened. The pain didn't vanish overnight but her relationship with it transformed. Week by week, the intensity began to lessen. She had stopped fighting the pain and had started listening to it. The body, in turn, softened. Sometimes, that is all it needs: to be seen, not resisted.

So what, really, is presence? It is not passive acceptance or doing nothing. It is an active, embodied awareness of what is. It is the willingness to be with what is true, without rushing to change it or judge it. It is feeling your breath move in and out, noticing the tension in your shoulders, hearing the subtle background sounds of life and allowing it all. Presence is about meeting yourself, moment by moment, with kindness and curiosity. Even if the moment holds discomfort or pain, presence allows space for transformation. Because only what we are willing to feel, can begin to heal.

For those new to cultivating presence, simple tools can help. One of the most effective is the **5-4-3-2-1 grounding technique**. When anxiety, panic, or physical symptoms flare, gently bring your attention to your senses:

- Name five things you can see
- Four things you can touch
- Three things you can hear
- Two things you can smell
- One thing you can taste or feel internally

This technique redirects the mind from imagined threats to the actual moment, where your body is always located.

Another powerful anchor is **mindful breathing**. For just three minutes, breathe in for a count of four, hold for two, and exhale for six. Focus only on the breath. When thoughts arise–and they will–gently return your attention to the inhale and exhale. The breath, always happening in the now, becomes your refuge.

Or try a short **"Here and Now" body scan**. Lie down and bring awareness to each part of your body; your feet, legs, belly, chest, shoulders, jaw. Notice what sensations arise: tightness, warmth, tingling. You are not trying to fix anything. You are simply offering presence. In this non-judgmental witnessing, the body often responds with a deep sense of safety and calm.

For those ready to go deeper, daily **Vipassana meditation** offers a profound path into presence. Practiced for centuries, Vipassana teaches the art of observing sensations without attachment or aversion. One hour a day can create lasting shifts in the nervous system, cultivating resilience and clarity from within.

So why does the present moment heal? Because it liberates us from the emotional charge of the past, and from the fearful projections of the future. It allows the mind and body to reconnect, to become allies once more. It helps us hear the body's subtle language; signs, symptoms, needs that are often drowned out by mental noise. And perhaps most importantly, it reminds us: **"Right now, I am alive. Right now, I am breathing. Right now, I can choose peace."** Even when pain exists, peace can coexist alongside it. They are not mutually exclusive.

In my years as a physician, I have witnessed this over and over. Some patients, though severely ill on paper, radiated calm, acceptance, and awareness. Their healing was faster, their outcomes more favorable. Others, seemingly healthy in reports, remained trapped in cycles of fear, resistance, and overthinking. They continued to suffer. The difference wasn't always biological but it was relational. Their relationship with the present moment defined the trajectory of their healing.

So if you're reading this now, I invite you: pause. Take a deep breath. Feel your body, its weight, its sensations, its aliveness. Feel the present moment holding you. Whisper gently to yourself:

"This moment is safe.
This moment is enough.
This moment is where I begin again."

Let healing begin not in some far-off future or buried past but here, now, in this breath.

Coming Up Next...

*In the next chapter, we'll dive into the role of **belief systems**, how what we think about illness, health, medicine, and ourselves **becomes a self-fulfilling prophecy**, influencing both outcomes and experiences.*

Because how we see our illness shapes how we live with it... and beyond it.

CHAPTER XVI

Belief system – The Power of Inner Narratives in Health

"The body listens to every story the mind tells."

This is almost the 3rd chapter on BELIEF. By this you can understand the importance of belief system in our health and illness.

As a physician, I've encountered countless patients over the years, many of whom have come in with the same medical diagnosis like diabetes, hypertension, autoimmune conditions, or chronic pain syndromes. Yet despite identical lab results, medications, or treatment plans, their healing trajectories often looked nothing alike. Some improved rapidly, defying expectations. Others, though seemingly stable medically, remained stagnant or even deteriorated. This discrepancy often had less to do with medicine and more to do with something invisible but profoundly influential, their **belief system.**

Beliefs are not passive thoughts floating in our minds. They are powerful, biologically active instructions. When someone repeatedly tells themselves, "I'm not going to get better," the body registers this as stress, hopelessness, and contraction. Conversely, when someone deeply believes, "I am healing. My body is working for me," a completely different set of physiological reactions occur, rooted in calm, hope, and balance. These beliefs, whether limiting or liberating, become internal narratives that shape not only a person's mental state but also their **biochemical reality.**

At the core of this process lies a powerful chain reaction. Thoughts evoke emotions. Emotions, in turn, trigger complex biochemical responses. Over time, these responses lay down patterns in the body either supporting health or feeding disease. Chronic stress, guilt, shame, or hopelessness can dysregulate hormonal systems, suppress immunity, disrupt digestion, and impair sleep. On the other hand, emotions like trust, joy, and optimism promote hormonal balance, cellular repair, and immune resilience. In this way, our **inner dialogue becomes our outer biology**.

Consider this: a belief is simply a repeated thought accepted as truth. It doesn't have to be logical or evidence-based, it just needs to feel familiar and emotionally reinforced. Many patients unconsciously carry beliefs like, "This illness is punishment," or "It runs in my family, so I'm doomed." These beliefs don't emerge from nowhere. They are shaped by childhood experiences, cultural attitudes, family history, and previous medical encounters. Yet once embedded, they can become invisible forces holding a person back from healing.

One of my patients, Raghubhai, a 52-year-old man with type 2 diabetes, arrived in my clinic already resigned to his fate. "My father had diabetes," he told me. "He died young. I know I will too." His belief wasn't based on blood sugar levels or complications. It was rooted in emotional inheritance, a story passed down and internalized without question. I could see how this narrative of inevitability was draining his vitality. We addressed his medications and lifestyle, of course, but we also worked deeply on his mindset. I asked him, "What if you became the first in your family to break this cycle?" This opened a door in his mind. He began to adopt a new perspective: "This is my opportunity to live better, not end the same way." Gradually, his blood sugars began to stabilize, but more importantly, his demeanor shifted. His energy returned. He laughed more. And the cloud of fear that had hung over him began to lift. This was not a placebo. It was a biological **transformation through belief.**

Most people are unaware of the beliefs they carry about their health. They may have unconsciously absorbed ideas like "I'm just not a healthy person," or "No treatment ever works for me," or worse, "Maybe I deserve this illness." These beliefs often come from childhood messaging, the media's portrayal of illness, religious or cultural conditioning, or even from comments made by medical professionals in moments of insensitivity. Left unexamined, these narratives create a lens through which all symptoms are interpreted, and they silently sabotage the healing process.

To shift these inner narratives, the first step is **awareness**. Ask yourself: What do I believe about this condition? What do I think it says about who I am? Is this belief fact or just a story I've gotten used to? Awareness is the first form of medicine. Once the story is seen, it can be questioned. The next step is to **consciously choose a new belief**. This isn't about positive thinking for its own sake. It's about **reframing reality** in a way that supports healing. Instead of "I'll never be okay," you might say, "My body is trying to heal, and I'm learning how to support it." Instead of asking "Why me?" ask "What is this illness trying to teach me about my life, my choices, or my priorities?"

Lastly, repetition with emotion is key. The subconscious mind doesn't respond to logic alone but it responds to **emotionally charged repetition.** This is why affirmations, visualizations, compassionate self-talk, and mindful practices are so powerful. When you say to yourself daily, "I am healing," and pair it with calm breathing or gratitude, your body begins to align with that frequency. This is not magic. This is a mental **rehearsal for physiological change**.

As a physician, I've evolved in how I engage with patients. I no longer stop at symptom checklists or diagnostic reports. I ask deeper questions: "What do you believe about this illness?" "What did your parents believe about health and healing?" "Do you feel worthy of recovery?" Because I've learned that without addressing the **inner story**, even the best medicine may fall short. Conversely, when the story begins to shift, even small interventions can yield profound results.

If you're reading this now....

I invite you to pause and reflect. What stories about your body, your health, your worthiness are you still carrying? Are these stories truly yours or inherited scripts from your past? And most importantly, **can you choose to write a new narrative**?

Tell yourself:

"I am not my diagnosis.

I am not my history.

I am a living system capable of renewal and healing."

Coming Up Next...

In the following chapter, we will explore how relationships, especially with those closest to us, impact our capacity to heal. Chronic illness rarely exists in a vacuum. It is shaped, sustained, or softened by the emotional ecosystems we live in every day.

CHAPTER XVII

Healing Together – Relationships, Boundaries, and Emotional Energy in Illness

"Sometimes, healing begins not with a pill, but with a conversation... or a boundary."

As a physician, I have witnessed the limits of purely biomedical treatment more times than I can count. Patients come in with chronic ailments like migraines, irritable bowel, autoimmune flares, fatigue syndromes and they are often deeply compliant. They take every prescribed medication, adhere to strict diets, ingest an arsenal of supplements, and attend follow-ups with great diligence. Yet, they continue to suffer. The healing doesn't come. The symptoms may shift, but true wellness eludes them. Then, almost always casually, a patient will offer a revealing aside: "My husband doesn't believe I'm really sick." Or "I can't rest, I have to take care of everyone else." Sometimes it's whispered, "I feel guilty asking for help." Or a quiet admission, "I'm always walking on eggshells at home."

These aren't just emotional footnotes to a medical history. They are energetic disturbances; chronic, often invisible stressors that live within the nervous system, within relationships, and within the very field of healing. Chronic illness, we must remember, does not exist in isolation. It exists within the ecology of the human experience, and often, that ecology includes entangled relationships, unmet emotional needs, suppressed voices, and histories of pain never fully acknowledged.

The Hidden Energy of Relationships

Each relationship in our lives, be it marital, parental, familial, friendly, or professional, carries an energetic charge. Some nourish us, infusing us with safety, love, and encouragement. Others drain us, leaving us depleted, anxious, or silently resentful. And many trap us in a chronic state of emotional hypervigilance, where we are constantly adapting, pleasing, hiding, or enduring. Over time, the nervous system accommodates these roles. The sympathetic branch remains on alert. The parasympathetic healing response is delayed or disrupted. Cortisol stays high. Sleep becomes shallow. Digestion falters. Hormones misfire. The immune system becomes dysregulated.

Our biology is not deaf to our relationships but it is shaped by them.

Case Study: When a Migraine Was Really a Message

Meera, a 39-year-old woman, came to me after years of suffering from disabling migraines. She had already visited top neurologists, undergone brain imaging, and tried a multitude of pharmacological and alternative treatments. Yet nothing offered lasting relief. In one of our longer integrative sessions, I gently asked, "Is there anything emotionally heavy going on in your life right now?" She paused. Then she reveals.

"I can't say no to my family," she confessed. "I'm exhausted. I haven't had a single day to myself in years."

Her migraines, we discovered, were often triggered during times of overwhelming responsibility like festivals, family events, caregiving episodes. We came to see her symptoms not as defects to suppress, but as signals to decode. Her body was articulating what her words never had: "I need space. I need to stop. I need help."

With that awareness, she began therapy. She started saying no to non-urgent demands, carving out personal time, asserting herself without apology. Three months later, she reported that her migraines had decreased by 70%. It wasn't a new drug that changed her life. It was a new relationship with herself, with her limits, with her right to say no.

Boundaries: The Medicine We're Not Taking often

In homoeopathic medical school, I learned not only about the structure of the cell, the biochemistry of disease, and the pharmacology of treatment. But also to ask: "Where in your life do you feel overwhelmed?" or "Whose emotions are you carrying that aren't yours?" or "Do you feel safe to say no?" I ask these questions often because I have been taught deep case taking skills. It's not easy to get mental symptoms or emotions from patients, it takes hours of case taking and multiple sessions. In this book I have described it shortly considering the length of chapters.

Boundaries are not walls. They are not rejections. They are the quiet, firm declarations of how we deserve to be treated. To the body, boundaries register as safety. When we uphold our boundaries, we signal to our nervous system: "I'm not in danger. I am allowed to rest. I am allowed to be." That's when the healing mechanisms of the body like rest, repair and regeneration begin to activate in full.

Relationship Patterns That Disrupt Healing

Through years of clinical observation and therapeutic conversations, I have come to identify several common relational patterns that can quietly perpetuate illness:

The Chronic Caretaker

This person habitually puts others before themselves, often to the point of depletion. They feel guilty resting. They apologize for saying no. Their worth becomes entangled with their service. Their body, eventually, begins to protest.

The Emotional Absorber

These are the emotional individuals who are hyper-attuned to the moods of those around them. They internalize others' distress, often without realizing it. Poor energetic boundaries lead to emotional exhaustion and somatic symptoms.

The Invisible One

Sometimes, illness becomes the only avenue through which a person feels seen or cared for. This is not manipulation but it is often a tragic compensation for unmet emotional needs from childhood or trauma.

The Fearful Receiver

These individuals have difficulty accepting support. Vulnerability feels dangerous. They feel undeserving of love or rest, and so they unconsciously push away help even when they need it most.

It's important to understand that these patterns are not flaws. They are survival strategies, shaped by earlier environments where needs were unmet or boundaries were unsafe. But in adulthood, when left unexamined, these adaptations can block the body's path to recovery.

Healing Through Relational Awareness

Healing requires more than medication. It requires energetic hygiene and emotional honesty. Here are ways to begin:

1. Audit Your Energy Daily

At the end of each day, reflect on your relationships. Ask:

- Who gave me energy today?
- Who drained me?
- What boundary did I uphold or betray?

This isn't about assigning blame. It's about cultivating awareness. Where awareness goes, healing follows.

2. Communicate Authentically

Learn to speak your truth, even when it trembles:

- "I need rest. I hope you'll understand."
- "I can't take that on right now."
- "I love you, but this is hurting me."

These are hard conversations but they are healing ones. When you express yourself honestly, your body no longer has to hold your pain for you.

3. Seek Support, Not Just Treatment

Healing is not meant to be solitary. Therapy, support groups, emotionally intelligent friendships, and conscious communities can become vital medicines. Let your body know: you don't have to carry this alone anymore.

A Word to the Caregivers

To those who support someone with chronic illness, your presence matters deeply. Your belief in their pain, your patience, and your emotional steadiness are often more healing than any supplement or surgery. And yet, your well-being matters too. You cannot pour from an empty cup. Make time for your own restoration. Healing is contagious, when one person in a relational field shifts, it creates ripple effects.

If You're Reading This...

Take a quiet moment. Think of your closest relationships. Ask yourself:

- Where do I feel safe to be my whole self?
- Where do I feel tension, guilt, or fear?
- What would change if I gave myself permission to rest, to speak, to ask?

Tell yourself: "I am allowed to take up space.
I am allowed to protect my peace.
I am allowed to heal even if others don't understand."

Because sometimes, the deepest healing act is simply this: choosing yourself, with love.

If this chapter resonates with you, you may also find comfort in the work of Dr. Bernie Siegel, particularly his book *"Love, Medicine and Miracles"*, which explores how love, belief, and emotional alignment often create unexpected paths to healing. His pioneering message echoes this truth: the body doesn't just need prescriptions but it needs emotional permission to thrive.

Coming Up Next...

In the next chapter, we will explore Life Purpose and Meaning in Chronic Illness. Because healing isn't merely the absence of symptoms. It's about rediscovering what makes life worth living.

CHAPTER XVIII

The Will to Heal – Purpose, Meaning, and the Inner Spark

"*Healing begins the moment life feels worth living again.*"

As physicians, we are trained with precision and discipline. We are taught to detect abnormalities, analyze lab reports, track biomarkers, adjust medications, and document progress in a language often devoid of emotion. Our focus is clear: diagnose, treat, manage. We are fluent in the language of pathology but often left tongue-tied when confronted with the soul's quiet cry for purpose.

Yet, over the years of treating chronic illness, I have come to realize that a question we rarely ask can sometimes matter more than any scan or blood test: **"Do you feel that your life has meaning?"**

This is not a philosophical indulgence. It is a biological necessity.

There is a powerful and often overlooked link between emotional vitality and physiological resilience. The human body does not exist in a vacuum; it thrives, struggles, or deteriorates based on the signals it receives, not just from the external environment, but from our internal world of meaning, purpose, and belief. The patients who reconnect with something to live for whether it be a loved one, a creative passion or a personal mission, often begin to heal in ways that science alone struggles to explain.

Why Purpose Matters in Chronic Illness

Purpose is not merely a psychological state, it has measurable physiological consequences. When someone loses their sense of purpose, when their days blur into a monotony of symptoms and appointments, the body responds. The nervous system becomes flat and unresponsive. The immune system becomes sluggish, less efficient. Inflammatory processes increase, fatigue becomes profound, and even adherence to medication wanes. The will to heal fades when the will to live is not engaged.

On the other hand, when meaning is reignited, even in a small way; the biological tide can turn. Neurotransmitters like dopamine and serotonin begin to rise, enhancing mood and motivation. The mind re-engages with life, and the body receives a new signal: "Life is still worth fighting for." This does not mean purpose cures disease outright, but it shifts the terrain–psychologically, neurologically, and immunologically toward healing.

Case Study: Rekindling the Spark

Consider the case of Shardaben, a 58-year-old woman who had been battling autoimmune arthritis for over a decade. She had knocked on every door, allopathic care, Ayurveda, Homoeopathy, alternative healing but nothing brought her lasting relief. She arrived in my clinic tired and in pain, but more than that, I noticed something deeper: a profound dullness in her gaze, as though life had dimmed its light inside her.

In our first conversation, I gently asked, "What brings you joy?"

She hesitated. "I don't remember," she whispered. "I used to love singing... before life got too busy."

With long conversation, I saw the root of her illness was not just autoimmune dysfunction but it was also soul-silencing. Along with the homoeopathic treatment plan, I gave her a different kind of prescription: "Sing again. Just five minutes a day."

At first, she felt awkward. But slowly, her voice returned not just physically, but spiritually. She began humming while cooking. She sang softly during her evening walk. Within weeks, something remarkable began to happen: her joint flares became less intense and less frequent. Her fatigue lessened. Her posture straightened. There was a new clarity in her eyes.

Pain had silenced her voice. Purpose helped her reclaim it.

Purpose Is Not Always Grand

There is a common myth that purpose must be heroic, that one must change the world, lead a movement, or achieve extraordinary success to live a meaningful life. But purpose is deeply personal and often humbly rooted. It might be tending a garden. Writing in a journal. Raising a child with love and patience. Volunteering an hour a week. Telling your story so someone else feels less alone. Or simply being fully present while sipping morning tea.

Healing does not always begin in hospitals or laboratories. Sometimes, it begins where meaning resides in the ordinary moments that remind us who we are and why we are here.

The Science of Meaning and Health

Modern research has begun to catch up with what ancient wisdom has long known: a sense of purpose is not only good for the soul but it is essential for the body.

Studies have consistently shown that individuals with a strong sense of meaning and direction in life experience:

- Lower levels of stress hormones like cortisol
- Stronger immune responses
- Quicker recovery from surgeries and illnesses
- Reduced markers of inflammation
- Greater resilience to chronic conditions such as cardiovascular disease and cancer
- Longer life spans and improved psychological well being

Purposeful living is now considered a health-promoting behavior, akin to regular exercise, a nutritious diet, and restful sleep. This is not a poetic metaphor, it is biochemistry. The biology of hope is real.

When Purpose Feels Lost

Chronic illness doesn't just affect the body, it alters identity. Many patients describe a grief that goes beyond pain:

"I'm not who I used to be."
"I can't do what I once loved."
"My life revolves around managing symptoms."

This erosion of identity can be as devastating as the illness itself. But purpose, like the body, is capable of regeneration. It may not look the same as it once did, but it can evolve.

Some patients find new meaning by mentoring others with similar diagnoses. Others become advocates for patient rights, or rediscover creativity they never had time to explore in their earlier years. Some turn inward, deepening spiritual or familial bonds. Illness may close one chapter, but it can also be the opening line of another.

A Simple Practice to Reconnect With Meaning

If you find yourself lost in the fog of illness or emotional fatigue, try this simple exercise I often share with patients; the "3 M's" Reflection:

1. **Moments**
   Recall three small moments from the past week that stirred your emotions, made you smile, cry, or feel truly alive.
2. **Meaning**
   Reflect on these moments: what do they say about what really matters to you?
3. **Movement**
   Choose one small, doable action that brings more of that feeling into your week.

This practice is not about dramatic change. It's about cultivating a quiet, steady sense of alignment with what makes life feel meaningful, right now, in the present moment.

If You're Reading This...

Ask yourself:

- What do I live for?
- What makes me feel like myself again, even if just for a few minutes?
- What have I always wanted to express, create, give, or explore?

And then say this out loud or write it down somewhere you'll see it:

"My illness is real, but so is my reason to keep going.
I still matter. I still have something to offer.
I am still here for a reason."

The body may falter. The path may be painful. But when the soul is lit with purpose, it can illuminate the road to healing in the darkest of times.

Coming Up Next....

In the next chapter, we'll explore the transformative power of self-expression. How suppressing our voice and creativity can manifest as illness, and how reclaiming them can become one of the most powerful prescriptions for healing.

CHAPTER XIX

Expression is Medicine – Creativity, Emotions, and the Art of Letting Go

As a doctor, I was trained to examine symptoms, diagnose conditions, and prescribe treatment. But as the years passed and the patients kept coming, often with persistent, unexplained, or recurring illnesses, I began to understand that true healing requires looking far beyond the boundaries of the physical body. I became more than a prescriber of medicine; I became a witness. A witness to stories unspoken, emotions unprocessed, and lives half-lived. The more I listened, the more it became clear: chronic illness, in many cases, is not merely a breakdown of physiology. It is a manifestation of what has been emotionally silenced and spiritually suppressed.

It took years of clinical experience and open-hearted conversations to realize how deeply our bodies bear the burden of our unexpressed inner worlds. The body is not separate from the mind, nor is it indifferent to our emotional state. In fact, it is one of our most honest communicators. When the heart cannot speak, the body does. It tells us through pain, through fatigue, through dysfunction what words never got the chance to say.

I recall vividly the story of Aarti, a woman in her late thirties, who came to me with persistent digestive issues. She had undergone multiple investigations, followed strict dietary changes, and tried various medications. Yet, her symptoms lingered. Something was missing. I decided to ask her not just about what she was eating, but about what was eating her. Her eyes welled up as she confessed, "I don't speak up. I keep peace. I swallow everything." And there it was. Her gut, an organ fundamentally responsible for breaking down and releasing had instead become a graveyard of emotion. She had been digesting the undigested: years of anger, disappointment, and silence.

We live in a culture that often misinterprets strength as emotional suppression. From a young age, many are taught that anger is dangerous, tears are embarrassing, joy must be controlled, and dreams must be sacrificed for practicality. Vulnerability becomes something to hide rather than honor. So, we adapt. We quiet our truths. We dim our desires. We learn to survive by becoming selectively numb. But these disowned parts of ourselves, our creative impulses, our raw emotions, our spontaneous expressions do not disappear. They go underground. And there, in the shadowy corners of our inner world, they begin to press against the body from within.

What becomes of the child who was told not to make noise, who never learned to cry without guilt? What happens to the teenager who had to be the "strong one" when their family fell apart? What becomes of the woman who gave up painting because life demanded she be practical? These parts do not vanish; they migrate. They take residence in the tight shoulders, the constricted throat, the knot in the stomach, the chronic fatigue, or the mysterious illness that no test can explain. The body becomes the storage unit for what the psyche cannot bear.

And yet, amid this silent suffering, I have also witnessed something extraordinary: the medicine of expression. The return to voice, to movement, to creation. I have seen patients transform not because of a new pill, but because they gave themselves permission to feel again. The moment a patient picks up a journal and writes without censoring; the first time they allow themselves to cry freely or scream into a pillow after years of restraint; when they dance behind closed doors or sing in the car with the windows rolled up, something vital shifts. They reconnect to their aliveness. And that shift is not decorative. It is deeply medicinal.

Expressive writing, for instance, has been shown to improve immune function and reduce doctor visits. Art therapy decreases cortisol levels and helps manage anxiety and trauma. Music therapy can stabilize heart rate and breathing patterns, especially in those suffering from PTSD or chronic stress. Even storytelling has been shown to regulate the nervous system and facilitate emotional integration. Why? Because when there is coherence between our inner and outer worlds, the body no longer needs to scream for attention.

But here's something crucial: expression does not have to be public to be powerful. You don't need to be an accomplished artist, a bestselling author, or a trained dancer to reclaim your emotional voice. Healing doesn't require a spotlight. It simply requires truth. You need only to give what's inside you a safe passage out, without shame, without judgment. Emotions, like water, are meant to move. When they stagnate, they become toxic. But when they are allowed to flow, they become purifying forces clearing, softening, and restoring balance within.

There is no universal prescription for expression. For some, it might be painting their grief in strokes of color. For others, it might be shouting into the wilderness or whispering into a diary. It could be cooking a dish that reminds you of a lost loved one, writing a letter you'll never send, or finally saying the words you needed to hear as a child. It may look like messy poetry, off-key singing, or awkward dancing, but none of it is irrelevant. In fact, these are the sacred rituals of self-return.

So if you have been ill for a long time, and your body feels like a mystery even to you, I gently invite you to ask:

- Have I silenced any part of myself to survive?
- Have I been holding it together for so long that I've forgotten how to fall apart?
- Could my symptoms be the language of something trying to be felt, seen, or released?

Let this chapter be your permission slip. Let it be the beginning of a return to your own voice. Write your rage with wild honesty. Paint your sorrow in blues and blacks. Sing your longing into the night air. Dance your fears into the ground beneath you. Cry your truth without apology. Because sometimes, your illness is not asking for more medication, but it's asking for more of you.

Healing, in its deepest form, is not just the absence of disease. It is the re-emergence of wholeness. And that wholeness begins when you are no longer hiding from others, from the world, or from yourself. Expression is not an accessory to healing. It is the medicine.

Expression Exercises: A Personal Prescription for Emotional Healing

These exercises are designed to gently guide you back into connection with your inner world. There is no right or wrong way to do them. The goal is not perfection, it's permission. Allow yourself to be honest, messy, raw, creative, and unfiltered. Let what's inside find its way out.

1. The Unsent Letter

Purpose: To express repressed emotions toward a person or situation (past or present).

- Write a letter to someone you never got to speak your truth to.
- Say everything you couldn't say then. Your anger, your hurt, your longing, your truth.
- Do not send it. This is for you, not them.

Try starting with: "What I never told you is…"
When you're done, tear it, burn it safely, or keep it as your ritual of release.

2. Creative Flow Time (20 Minutes)

Purpose: To reconnect with your innate creativity and voice.

Choose one:

- Paint with your fingers or a brush with no plan, no pressure.
- Free-write in a journal without editing or censoring.
- Dance to one powerful song with your eyes closed.
- Sing or hum a tune from childhood.

3. Body Release Practice

Purpose: To let your body express what words cannot.

- Set a timer for 5–10 minutes.
- Close the door, play music that matches your mood.
- Let your body move however it wants; shake, sway, stomp, curl up, punch a pillow, stretch, or collapse.
- Let sound come too: sighs, hums, screams, laughter, or tears.

Notice how your energy shifts afterward. This is your body recalibrating.

Try doing this once a week. Over time, notice how your emotional landscape shifts.

Coming Up Next...

In the next chapter, we'll explore the role of the environment in healing.

CHAPTER XX

The Healing Environment – Space, Silence, and the Nervous System

When I first began practicing medicine, my focus was almost exclusively on what was happening inside the body. I immersed myself in studying organs, systems, cells, and biochemistry. Every symptom, every pathology, was approached through the lens of internal dysfunction. Diagnosis led to prescription, prescription led to biochemical correction or so I believed. But over the years, something shifted. Patterns began to emerge that challenged this internal-only model. Two patients, both with the same diagnosis, of similar age, constitution, and on virtually identical treatment plans, would have drastically different outcomes. Initially, I searched for hidden physiological variables, assuming I must have missed a biological clue. But gradually, the truth became undeniable: the difference may often lay outside the body.

It wasn't always the medication that made the difference. It was the environment, both the outer world surrounding the patient and the inner world they inhabited emotionally and mentally. When you observe carefully, you will find that some lived in simple homes filled with natural light, the laughter of children, and a sense of warmth even if they had limited means. Others, despite material wealth, existed in emotionally charged, overstimulating, or cluttered environments and homes crowded not just with objects, but with unresolved grief, conflict, and chronic stress. Some were nurtured by families who intuitively created healing spaces through care and calm. Others were caught in what I came to call emotional noise, a constant background hum of anxiety, overstimulation, and pressure, where silence was a stranger and rest was elusive.

It became clear to me that **healing is not only about removing disease; it is about creating the conditions for peace**. Without peace, internal and external, the body struggles to repair. Without safety, the nervous system remains in a defensive stance, unable to fully surrender to the biological processes of restoration.

The Nervous System Needs Safety to Heal

The human nervous system is not a passive observer of its environment; it is deeply reactive, designed to assess safety continuously. This system is our ancient survival tool which monitors every flicker of light, every tone of voice, every moment of quiet or chaos, determining whether we are safe or under threat. And in today's world, subtle but chronic stressors abound: constant digital noise, emotional conflict, cluttered spaces, deadlines, unprocessed trauma, and the relentless expectation to be productive at all times.

All of these inputs keep the nervous system in a sympathetic, alert state, geared toward survival rather than restoration. In this state, the body becomes tense, the breath shallow, the digestive system compromised, and the inflammatory response heightened. Sleep becomes fractured. Healing, which requires a state of deep biological trust, is put on hold. But when the body perceives safety (when we enter a calm, clean, emotionally supportive space) the shift is almost magical. The parasympathetic nervous system takes the reins, activating the 'rest, digest, and repair' mode. Muscles soften. The heart finds a slower rhythm. Breathing deepens. In this sacred physiological state, the body begins to heal, not because of a pill, but because the environment whispers: "You're safe now."

Case Study: The Woman Who Couldn't Sleep

I remember Renukaben, a 45-year-old schoolteacher who had been battling chronic insomnia and fibromyalgia for years. Her case was one of my most frustrating initially. We tried everything: tranquilisers, magnesium, meditation apps, strict sleep hygiene, nutritional support. Yet, night after night, she tossed and turned, and each morning she woke in pain. One day, with weary eyes and a cracking voice, she said something that caught my attention: "Even when I lie down, I feel like the day is chasing me."

That metaphor struck a chord. I paused and asked her to describe her bedroom. She hesitated, then admitted it was filled with old boxes, school files, her children's scattered belongings, and her ever-present phone buzzing with late-night messages. "There's no silence," she said. "Not in my room. Not in my head." We made one shift, not a medical one, but an environmental one. I asked her to turn her bedroom into a sanctuary. She removed the clutter, boxed away the work files, and introduced soft, warm lighting. She began turning off all screens by 9 PM, kept her phone in another room, and replaced her pre-bed routine with short prayer, silence, and a few minutes of slow breathing. Within two weeks, her sleep deepened. Her pain lessened. Her nervous system had finally been given permission to exhale. Not through pharmacology but through peace.

The Elements of a Healing Environment

You don't need to live in an ashram or atop a Himalayan peak to experience healing. A healing environment is not defined by extravagance, it is defined by intention. Healing spaces are cultivated, not purchased. They are crafted through attention to the subtle forces that shape our physiology: light, sound, energy, and emotion.

1. Physical Space:

Decluttering is not just about aesthetics, it's about energy. A room filled with unnecessary objects becomes a room filled with unresolved stories and stuck energy. Start by simplifying. Create space to breathe, literally and metaphorically. Let in natural light. Invite the outdoors in with plants and fresh air. Surround yourself with colors that calm the mind, cool blues, soft whites, gentle greens. Most importantly, designate sacred spaces in your home where negativity is not welcome. Your bedroom, in particular, should be a sanctuary, not a battlefield.

2. Sensory Input:

We live in a world of overstimulation. The nervous system was never designed to process constant notifications, digital glare, and back-to-back stimuli. Reduce screen exposure, especially in the hours before sleep. Instead, fill your space with sounds that soothe, gentle instrumental music, the rustle of leaves, or the quiet rhythm of your own breath. Introduce scents that ground you: lavender, chamomile, sandalwood. Let your environment become a symphony of softness.

3. Emotional Vibration:

The emotional climate of a space is perhaps the most potent element. Avoid engaging in emotionally charged conversations especially in your resting areas. Reclaim silence as a healing tool. Even ten minutes of stillness can recalibrate a tired mind. Write affirmations of calm and place them where your eyes will fall on them each day. Most importantly, surround yourself with people who respect your peace. Emotional safety is as crucial as physical safety.

The Power of Silence

In our modern culture, silence is often seen as a void to be filled. We fear it. We escape from it. Yet, silence is the space in which the body hears its own wisdom. Silence is not emptiness, it is the womb of restoration. In silence, emotions can rise without judgment and release without force. The mind slows, the heart opens, and the body softens into trust. When my own days become chaotic, I retreat into stillness, not as a luxury, but as a necessity. Even five minutes of breath-focused silence can change the trajectory of a day. In that quiet, I return to myself. I remember who I am beneath the doing, beneath the noise. I understand the true value of silence during my Vipassana retreat. During 10 days of workshop we have to follow complete silence, even no eye contact with other fellows, it's known as *"Aaryamaun".* Which had a profound effect on me.

If You're Reading This...

Take a deep breath. Let it be slow, full, unforced. Then look around you. What in your space today invites calm? What agitates your senses or tightens your chest? When was the last time you truly sat in stillness, not to achieve something, but simply to be? Ask yourself: what does your nervous system need right now to feel safe?

You deserve to rest. You deserve beauty, peace, and simplicity. You deserve a space that reflects your inner longing for safety and stillness. Because healing doesn't just happen inside cells, it unfolds in the space between them. It happens in the breath between thoughts, in the pause before sleep, in the moment your body finally says: I can let go.

Coming Up Next...

In the next chapter, we'll explore **role of a physician–beside prescriptions**

CHAPTER XXI

The Doctor as Healer – From Prescription to Presence

From Solving to Serving

I write the whole chapter in bold letters to highlight the importance of the role of a physician over medicine.

When I first received my medical degree, I was filled with pride, armed with protocols, and infused with purpose. My white coat symbolized knowledge, my stethoscope a badge of competence. Like many of my peers, I had been rigorously trained to identify symptoms, reach a diagnosis, and prescribe the right treatment. The formula was simple: Problem → Diagnosis → Prescription → Cure. But actually, in many times its not cure but relief from symptoms.

Andso I practiced.

For years, I immersed myself in clinical logic, investigative questioning, and biochemical pathways. I trusted lab reports, imaging studies, and the efficacy rates outlined in peer-reviewed journals. I was diligent, evidence-based, and methodical.

But something always felt incomplete.

Despite following every clinical step correctly, I noticed that some patients didn't improve. Others returned with different symptoms, their pain migrating from one part of the body to another. And some appeared to suffer from conditions for which medicine had no precise name like chronic fatigue, fibromyalgia, irritable syndromes. Over time, a deeper truth began to emerge: my patients weren't just handing me symptoms, they were handing me stories.

Stories of grief that had never been expressed. Stories of betrayal buried under years of chronic inflammation. Stories of anxiety cloaked in the language of arrhythmias. And, most of all, stories of people trying to be heard in a system that often only measured what could be tested.

It was then I realized something profound: healing does not begin when a prescription is written but it begins the moment we become fully present.

Beyond the Tools: The Art of Presence

In modern medicine, much of our identity as physicians is wrapped in symbols, the white coat, the stethoscope, the jargon. These are the external signs of authority and competence. But the role of a true healer is far more intimate and expansive.

A healer is not just a technician of the body, they are a witness of the soul.

Over the years, there were countless moments when I had no miracle drug to offer, no surgical solution to suggest. Yet, when I chose to sit beside my patients, to listen without interrupting, to allow silence to stretch without filling it with solutions, something began to shift.

I remember one particular patient, who was in my relation, an elderly woman bedridden with advanced rheumatoid arthritis. Her joints were stiff, her spirit was weary. No pharmacological regimen had offered significant relief. I visited her regularly, often with nothing more than my presence to offer. I would sit by her bedside, hold her hand, and listen. We spoke not about inflammation markers or joint counts, but about her garden, her childhood dog, her regrets, and her long-lost love.

One afternoon, she said with quiet tears, "You're the first person who's really seen me in years." That week, she asked to sit up in bed again. The pain remained, but something deeper had moved, something medicine alone could not touch.

It was then I learned: sometimes, what a patient needs most is not to be cured, but to be seen.

The Neuroscience of Human Connection

While these insights may sound poetic or "soft," contemporary science confirms what traditional healers and ancient systems have always known: connection heals.

Recent studies in psychoneuroimmunology, interpersonal neurobiology, and relationship-centered care have demonstrated the biological effects of empathy and presence:

- Empathy improves clinical outcomes. Patients recover faster, adhere better to treatment, and report higher satisfaction when they feel genuinely heard and understood.
- Active listening reduces stress biomarkers. Both physicians and patients experience reductions in cortisol and inflammatory markers when interactions are compassionate and attentive.

- Voice tone matters. Research shows that a physician's vocal warmth can influence patient trust, adherence, and even pain perception.
- Body language shapes biology. Eye contact, open posture, and attentiveness trigger parasympathetic responses in patients, helping them shift from survival mode to healing mode.

This is not sentimentalism, it is neurobiology. It is the body's response to being held, not just physically, but emotionally and spiritually. Presence is not an extra; it is essential.

Who Heals Whom?

There exists a quiet paradox in the world of medicine: while doctors often believe we are the ones doing the healing, the truth is, we are healed in the process, too.

Each patient who walks through our doors carries more than a condition. They carry wisdom. They teach us about resilience, vulnerability, and the courage it takes to confront illness. Their stories enrich us, expand us, and humble us.

Over time, I stopped seeing myself as the expert above the patient and began to view the healing encounter as a sacred partnership. The patient is not a passive recipient of care, but an active co-creator in the healing journey. They bring their history, intuition, energy, and agency. I bring my training, presence, and care.

Healing, in its truest sense, is a co-created space of trust and meaning. In that space, both doctor and patient are transformed.

From Fixing to Holding

Medical training conditions us to fix. We are rewarded for diagnoses, praised for interventions, admired for decisiveness. Yet, not all suffering can be fixed. Not all pain is meant to be erased. Some pain is calling to be witnessed, not removed.

Now, before every consultation, I ask myself three questions:

1. Can I meet this person beyond their diagnosis?
2. Can I listen for what is not being said?
3. Can I hold their pain without rushing it away?

Because sometimes, healing is not a "cure." It is the integration of what once felt unbearable. It is the reclaiming of wholeness. It is peace, even in the presence of symptoms.

A Call to My Fellow Physicians and Caregivers

To those walking this path of healing alongside me, as medical doctors, therapists, nurses, holistic practitioners, I offer this invitation:

- When was the last time you truly slowed down to connect?
- Have you kept your sense of wonder, or have you fallen into autopilot?
- Can you return to the soul of medicine, not just its science?

We must remember: people don't come to us only for pills and procedures. They come for reassurance, for clarity, for hope. They come to feel less alone in their suffering.

Let us not become so focused on the disease that we forget the person.

Let us prescribe presence as generously as we prescribe medications.

Let us become healers, not just practitioners.

To the Reader Seeking Healing

And if you are reading this chapter as someone walking through illness, as a patient, a seeker, a survivor, please hear this:

You are not your symptoms. You are not a case number or a collection of lab values. You are a human being with a story, with energy, with inner wisdom.

You are allowed to ask for more than just medical treatment. You are allowed to seek a healer who sees you wholly, your body, your emotions, your dreams, your fears.

Do not settle for less.

Choose a doctor who listens with their whole being, not just their clipboard. Ask for presence, not just prescriptions. You are worthy of that kind of care.

You are not broken. You are becoming.

Let Our Presence Be the First Prescription

In the end, the most powerful tool we have is not our pen or protocol but our presence.

Let it be the first medicine we offer, the silent balm we bring, the foundation on which all healing rests.

Let us heal–and be healed–through the sacred act of showing up.

125

Books From Which I Have Got The Insights.

Organon of medicine - by Dr Samual Hahnemann

The Power of your subconscious mind -by Joseph Murphy

Biology of Beliefs -by Bruice Lipton

Love, Medicine and Miracles -by Bernie Siegel

You can heal your life -by Louise L Hay

Energy Healing -by Abby Wynne

The wisdom of the body -by Walter B Cannon

Ageless body, Timeless mind -by Deepak Chopra

Jaage Antarbodh -by Shree satyanarayana Goenka

What doctors Don't get to study in medical school -by B M Hegde

Visualization -by Jitendra Adhia

The secret -by Rhonda Byrne

Prerna nu zarnu -by Jitendra Adhia

You are the placebo -by Dr Joe Dispenza

Breaking the habit of being yourself -by Dr Joe Dispenza

Mind - Body medicine -by Dr Alan Watkins

The body keeps the score -by Dr Bessel van der Kolk

Molecules of Emotion -by Candace B Pert